Leah Kunkle Acus, Ph.D., received a doctoral degree in education from Michigan State University. Dr. Acus directs a program that she developed for preschool children, lectures to parent groups, and is active in teacher-training seminars.

LEAH KUNKLE ACUS

QUARRELING KIDS

Stop the Fighting and Develop Loving
Relationships Within the Family

4111 — Feb. 1992

A SPECTRUM BOOK

Prentice-Hall, Inc., *Englewood Cliffs, New Jersey 07632*

Library of Congress Cataloging in Publication Data

ACUS, LEAH KUNKLE.
   Quarreling kids.

   (A Spectrum Book)
   Bibliography: p. 198
   Includes index.
   1. Child development. 2. Brothers and sisters. 3. Quarreling. I. Title.
HQ772.A154   306.8'7   80-28474
   ISBN 0-13-748012-1
   ISBN 0-13-748004-0 (pbk.)

Editorial/production supervision and interior design by Suse L. Cioffi
Interior illustrations by L.A. Hoedema
Manufacturing buyer: Cathie Lenard

This Spectrum Book can be made available to businesses and organizations at a special discount when ordered in large quantities. For more information contact:

Prentice-Hall, Inc.
General Book Marketing
Special Sales Division
Englewood Cliffs, New Jersey 07632

10 9 8 7 6 5 4 3 2 1

Printed in the United States of America

PRENTICE-HALL INTERNATIONAL, INC., *London*
PRENTICE-HALL OF AUSTRALIA PTY. LIMITED, *Sydney*
PRENTICE-HALL OF CANADA, LTD., *Toronto*
PRENTICE-HALL OF INDIA PRIVATE LIMITED, *New Delhi*
PRENTICE-HALL OF JAPAN, INC., *Tokyo*
PRENTICE-HALL OF SOUTHEAST ASIA PTE. LTD., *Singapore*
WHITEHALL BOOKS LIMITED, *Wellington, New Zealand*

dedicated to:

David, my husband who encourages me to grow and become.

Scott, our sixteen-year-old son who long ago said, "Love is when you bring your mommy trees."

Cathy, our eleven-year-old daughter who said, "A friend is someone who loves you even when you're dirty."

Carrie, our six-year-old daughter who said, "The day before tomorrow is a wonderful day."

Linda, our infant daughter who didn't say anything but patiently waited to be born until three days after the completion of this book.

contents

acknowledgments

I offer my sincere gratitude and appreciation to those who have given so generously of their time, encouragement, and knowledge in helping to make this book possible: Dr. Louise Sause (a wonderful teacher whose words are always with me), Wendy Wallace, Rosana Weber, Georgia Bentley, Dr. David Acus, Joanne Smith, Dr. Jon Herbener, Frances Parrott, Joyce Kunkle, Sandra Witt, Pinehill Nursery School Staff (Barbara Foor, Candace Hoffman, Cinda Martin, Marcia Geise, Connie Hayne, Wendy Gillette), Reva Snyder, Mitzi Dimmers, Sue Whitaker, and the many parents and children who have shared their personal experiences with me.

Photo credits: Scott Acus, Cathy Acus, Carrie Acus, Andrew Smith, Susan Smith. Illustrations by L.A. Hoedema.

preface

Carol hurriedly packs her three children into the car, reminding them to keep their feet off each other's clean clothes. They are going to the photographer for their annual sibling photograph. The children smile and look lovingly at one another as the photographer snaps them from all angles. Carol hopes there will be an attractive picture for the family album showing what loving relationships exist among these children.

On the way home from the studio, the children act less loving toward one another. They fight over who will get to sit next to the window, whose foot touches whose clean white socks, and whether the passing car is "tan!" "beige!" or "light brown!"

A few weeks later the pictures arrive. Mother and Father

are pleased with the angelic faces and warm, loving sibling relationships depicted in one of the photos. As they proudly place the picture in the album Father remarks, "It's too bad they can't look like this more often around the house. They seem to quarrel a lot more than they act loving toward one another."

This father expresses the feelings of many parents who try to create a loving, peaceful home environment for their children, yet are sometimes puzzled by their children's quarreling and fighting:

> *"I know my kids love each other so why do they have to fight so much?"*
>
> *"When I try to break up their fights, I usually just end up making matters worse. Should I just let them fight it out for themselves?"*
>
> *"If a little quarreling among children is OK, at what point does it become harmful to them?"*
>
> *"How can I decrease the amount and intensity of fighting that goes on among my children, short of locking them in separate rooms?"*

A major premise of this book is that children who possess positive self-concepts can and will develop warm, loving sibling relationships within the family. *Part One* of *QUARRELING KIDS* examines the *types* of quarrels engaged in by children, and discusses the many reasons *why* brothers and sisters quarrel. *Part Two* discusses the development of children's self-concepts and offers concrete, practical suggestions to parents as to how they can help their children:

1. acquire self-concepts which are more positive;
2. develop warm, loving sibling relationships;
3. reduce the amount and intensity of sibling quarrels.

part I

Quarreling: Why do Siblings Quarrel?

chapter 1

Quarreling

Sound familiar? We can all recall similar squabbles occurring in our own homes, perhaps as recently as five minutes ago. The average parent with typical children can undoubtedly offer a half dozen more examples of siblings' quarreling. While compiling material for *Quarreling Kids,* I spoke with many parents who contributed personal examples of sibling quarrels. Although these parents did not always agree as to why children quarrel or what to do about quarreling, they were in unanimous agreement on one point–quarrels among siblings are much more common in most homes, than the common cold. Unfortunately, knowing that all your neighbors suffer with common colds doesn't make your own cold any less annoying. Likewise, knowing that your neighbors have children who quarrel does not ease the frustration of having to listen to your own children quarrel, while thinking, "I wonder if all this quarreling is good for my children or is it actually hurting them?"

IS QUARRELING HARMFUL TO CHILDREN?

The effect of quarreling on children depends on several factors: the *kinds of quarrels* they are involved in, the *amount of quarreling* they do, and the *emotional intensity of their quarreling.* The way siblings quarrel, how often they quarrel, and how angry they become varies greatly among families.

In some homes children seldom quarrel and their quarrels are brief. The children don't viciously attack each other physically or with words and they do not suffer long-term harmful effects from quarrels. At the other extreme, some children quarrel non-stop, and often are hostile in their attacks upon each other. Their quarrels may include shoving, biting, shouting, hair-pulling, name calling, and "put-downs" of each other's personal character. This kind of quarreling *is* harmful to children.

TYPES OF QUARRELING

We shall look at three types of quarrels to determine the likelihood of harmful effects on children caused by each.

Nuisance Quarrels

Most noisy quarrels which don't necessarily result in serious damage to children are still a nuisance to parents. All families have nuisance quarrels. Nuisance quarrels often occur late at night in the back seat of the family car on the way home from Grandpa and Grandma's house, or just before dinner as the parent rushes to complete the meal for the starving family. Following is an example of a typical nuisance quarrel. The basis for such quarrels is the fact that the children are in bad moods due to hunger, tiredness, boredom, or other temporary conditions.

Nuisance quarrels can be turned on and off by children as though they were controlled by a switch, to which, unfortunately, the parents do not have access. It is truly amazing how these nuisance quarrels can be replaced instantly by civilized, loving, constructive sibling conversation. Nuisance

Nuisance Quarrel

quarrels are difficult for parents to follow. It is nearly impossible to figure out who started the fight or why it began. Parents who attempt to mediate in such quarrels quickly discover that children involved in them are not capable of logically negotiating settlements. The wise parent stays cool and collected in the midst of such a quarrel, realizing that this type of quarrel has nothing to do with how much the children love each other.

Verbal Debate Quarrels

Some quarrels may be beneficial to children. Such quarrels can be called "verbal debate quarrels." In verbal debate quarrels the children disagree concerning a particular topic and use their accumulated knowledge and logic to try to persuade the other of their particular point of view. These debates can be valuable settings for learning, if they focus on the topic of disagreement rather than attacking each other's personal character. If during and after such debates the children continue to respect each other and their rights to have different points of view on a topic, these quarrels are not harmful to children. The following is a verbal debate quarrel:

Verbal Debate Quarrel

Some verbal debate quarrels which begin on the right track, by offering children an opportunity to discuss a topic of interest, become sidetracked and end up becoming quarrels full of personal attacks on each other. At this time, the verbal debate ceases to be beneficial to children. The quarrel turns into another type of quarrel, the destructive quarrel, which can be harmful to children.

Destructive Quarrels

The content of destructive quarrels can cause long-term emotional damage to children. In such quarrels, children attack each other with great hostility. The attack may be physical, including hitting, kicking, hair-pulling, and biting. Or, the hostility may be shown verbally, through shouting, name-calling, and degrading of each other's personal character. Destructive quarrels are obviously the most harmful to children.

Destructive Quarrel

From the chart on the next page, it is evident that all quarrels are not the same. *Quarrels vary in cause, focus, expression, and effect on the participants.*

All children quarrel to some extent. If children's quarrels

THREE TYPES OF QUARRELS

	NUISANCE QUARRELS	*VERBAL DEBATE QUARRELS	DESTRUCTIVE QUARRELS
Cause of Quarrel	temporary irritability	healthy desire to use one's knowledge to exchange information on a topic of interest	feelings of inadequacy (low self-esteem)
Focus of Quarrel	trivia, making mountains out of molehills	a topic of mutual interest	personal character of participants
Expression of Quarrel	verbal bickering, picking, needling	verbal exchange of information, willingness to listen to different points of view	shouting, biting, shoving, name-calling, degrading of personal character
Effect of Quarrel on Children	short-term anger vented on sibling with no resulting long-term damage to children	practice in verbal communication and sharing of ideas	possible long-term emotional damage to children

*Verbal debate quarrels are defined in this chapter. However, due to the focus of verbal debate quarrels they are not to be considered harmful to children and should not be discouraged. The remainder of Part I will focus exclusively on the "nuisance" and "destructive" types of quarrels.

are of the nuisance type and do not dominate the day's activities, there is little need for great concern. Verbal debate quarrels, which are not harmful and focus on a topic of disagreement, can provide learning settings with desirable benefits to children. Destructive quarrels, however, can seriously harm children and should be eliminated.

CAN PARENTS HELP THEIR CHILDREN LEARN TO QUARREL LESS?

Informed, sensitive parents can play an important role in helping their children learn to quarrel less and replace quarreling with warm, constructive sibling relationships. The first step in helping our children lessen the amount and the intensity of their quarreling is to understand *why* they quarrel. Nuisance and destructive quarrels are *symptoms* of underlying problems, some serious, others less so.

Consider the physician treating a sick child. He notes the child's fever as a symptom, but focuses on the underlying illness. The fever signals that something is not right with the child. The physician knows that eliminating the real problem (the illness) will rid the child of the fever (symptom). Eliminating only the fever does not necessarily mean the illness is gone.

Similarly, nuisance and destructive quarrels are symptoms which signal parents that something is not right with the child. Parents should concentrate on eliminating the underlying problem. When the underlying problem is cured, the symptoms of quarreling will lessen automatically. If parents focus only on getting rid of the quarreling such as demanding that quarreling stop, the underlying cause of that quarreling may continue to act as a negative force against the child's emotional well-being.

Children's quarrels should be listened to carefully as

their quarrels can provide us with useful information about
how children feel about the world around them and about
themselves. We may discover by listening to our children's
quarrels that they need more attention, feel jealous of each
other, are having difficulty with their peers, are being overly
pressured to achieve, are imitating our own undesirable
behavior, have poor self-concepts, feel insecure, and much
more.

chapter 2

Sibling Rivalry

Early one morning, five–year–old Karen asks her mother if she can put her toothbrush next to her mother's. Mother, half asleep and not yet capable of anticipating the dire consequences of such a momentous decision, replies, "Sure, honey." Karen happily re-arranges the family toothbrushes. Then, her nine-year-old sister Joyce walks in. We hear:

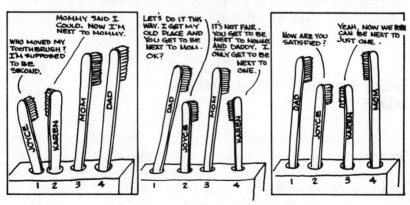

We can't help laughing a little at the absurdity of fighting over the arrangements of toothbrushes. However, beneath the surface of this quarrel, we find that the two sisters do not find the incident at all humorous. Joyce is serious about wanting to keep her toothbrush where it has always been, and Karen is serious in her desire "to be next to Mommy." It is also important to Karen that her sister not get to be next to *two* parents, if she can be next to only *one* parent. Karen is happy only when she and her sister get to share their parents equally. This is a typical example of "sibling rivalry" at work.

WHAT IS SIBLING RIVALRY?

Sibling rivalry is the competitive struggle which exists among brothers and sisters because of their desire to get their fair share of parental approval, attention, and love. When children do not receive what they perceive as their fair share, they become jealous of the attention and love given to their siblings.

Jealousy is one of the major causes of sibling rivalry. The amount of jealousy existing among siblings depends on how secure each child feels about his parents' love for him. Children whose desire and need for parental love is being fulfilled develop a minimum of jealousy toward their siblings, thus experiencing much less sibling rivalry.

DOES SIBLING RIVALRY EXIST IN ALL FAMILIES?

The answer is, probably, yes. However, the amount and intensity of children's jealousy varies greatly. In some families there are only minor and fleeting feelings of sibling jealousy. In other families there are long-term, intense feelings of jealousy among siblings.

FACTORS AFFECTING SIBLING RIVALRY AND QUARRELING

The photographs below show brothers and sisters from two different families. Knowing nothing about the children's individual personalities, or the quality of the children's interactions with their parents, which family would you predict might have more sibling conflict?

Studies on aggression, hostility, anger, and sibling relationships indicate that there is a relationship between these factors (age, sex, birth order, and spacing of children) and the amount and intensity of sibling conflicts. On the basis of this information alone, we can predict that the Allen family will probably have more sibling conflict than the Marshall family, as we will see.

If your family resembles the Allens, your first reaction might be, "Now you tell me. Obviously, I can't change my children's ages, sex, birth order or the number of years between them. Does this mean I am doomed to years of sibling battles?"

Fortunately, this parent is not doomed to a life as a

professional referee of children's battles. Although there is a relationship between the factors discussed and sibling quarrels, these factors are *potential* difficulties and by themselves do not cause sibling conflicts. Parents can take steps to greatly reduce the potential effects which these factors might have on sibling relationships, including helping their children feel good about the place they have in the family.

Birth Order as a Potential Factor Affecting Sibling Quarrels

Every position in the family has advantages and disadvantages. Being the oldest, youngest, or the middle child can be a difficult or a comfortable position depending upon how the child feels about his position.

Oldest Child. "Sometimes it isn't easy being the oldest child in the family because you think your parents expect more of you than your younger brothers and sisters." Studies confirm the suspicion that parents often have higher expectations for the oldest child and push him harder to achieve than they push younger siblings. The oldest child may feel that his brothers and sisters "get away with murder" and receive more attention than he does. A child who feels this way may reach the conclusion that his parents love his younger siblings more than they love him. When this occurs, the oldest child is likely to resent younger siblings and try to antagonize them.

Middle Child. "It isn't always easy being the middle child. Your parents seem to pay more attention to the oldest because he can do so many 'big' things. They pay attention to the youngest because she is so 'cute.' Sometimes you feel neglect-

Quarreling Instigated by the "Middle Child"

ed." Studies support this suspicion that middle children are more likely than the others to be neglected.

If the middle child feels neglected, whether actually neglected or not, he will probably reach the conclusion that his parents love his older and younger siblings more than they love him. Middle children may even seek their parents' attention by provoking negative attention from their parents. Children deprived of quality attention may conclude that negative attention is better than none at all.

Youngest Child. "There are times when it isn't easy being the youngest child in the family because you never get to do things your older brothers and sisters do. You can't stay up as late or get as much allowance as they do because they are older than you. Sometimes you think your parents really mean they are *better* than you. You think maybe Mom and Dad love your brothers and sisters more because they can do 'big' things. You also feel little because your brothers and sisters boss you around all the time and tease you a lot."

If the youngest child feels his parents love him less than his older siblings, he may try to put his siblings in a bad

Quarreling Instigated by the "Youngest Child"

light with his parents, for example, by screaming in faked pain when a sibling brushes by him.

Children's Sex as a Potential Factor Affecting Sibling Quarrels

Brothers fight with brothers, sisters fight with sisters, and brothers and sisters fight with each other. Regardless of children's sex, there will be sibling conflicts. Interesting, however, is the observation made by Brian Sutton-Smith that there is more conflict among same–sex siblings (Sutton-Smith, 1970). We can better understand why children of the same sex may be inclined to quarrel more when we listen to Stephen tell what it is like to have a brother who always seems to do things better than he can:

It's nice to have a brother because you have someone who likes to do things you like. But, it's bad too. When we run races, he always wins. When we play ball, he always gets more points.

When we play checkers, he wins—unless, I accidentally spill the board over. Then we tie.

The activities of children of the same sex are usually more similar than those of children of the opposite sex. Often, those activities involve competition in which there is a winner and a loser. Young children are not mature enough to handle competition well. When the child loses, he feels hurt and resentful and may attack the sibling who made him a loser.

Does this mean that just because siblings are of the same sex they are destined to a troubled relationship? Parents who realize that same-sex siblings often find themselves in competition with each other can help their children by lessening the number of competitive experiences available to them and encouraging cooperative experiences such as building a fort or outfitting a dollhouse. When competition is inevitable, parents can help children realize that both of them are loved regardless of their ability to win and that they are special and wonderful because of who they are, not because of what they can do in relation to anyone else.

Spacing as a Potential Factor Affecting Sibling Quarrels

After an unusually hectic weekend, Perry and Betty tuck Jimmy age 8, Todd age 6, and Holly age 4 into bed and retire to the sofa.

BETTY: Some weekend! Our kids fought the whole time. Why do they have to be at their worst when we have company?

PERRY: Do you really think it was that bad? All kids fight.

BETTY: Jane and Paul's three sure didn't. They didn't say a cross word to each other the whole time. And did you see how Matt helped Sheila up when he accidentally knocked her down? If one of our kids accidentally knocked the other down, there would be a big battle.

PERRY: You're forgetting something, Betty. Their children are five years apart and ours are so close in age. That makes a difference.

BETTY: Why does that make a difference?

PERRY: There's more to fight about when you are close in age because you all want the same things. When you are fifteen you don't really care whether your four-year-old brother hogs all the Matchbox cars. But if Todd tried to hog all the cars, David and Holly would both be upset because toy cars are important when you are four, six, and eight years old.

BETTY: I suppose you're right. If we had wanted a quiet house we should have spaced our children twenty years apart.

Perry is accurate in his observation that one of the reasons children who are close in age quarrel more is because they have more about which to quarrel. Children further apart in age have less opportunity to establish a common battle ground. The ten-year-old isn't likely to fight with her four-year-old sister over a tricycle. But a five-year-old won't hesitiate to fight with his four-year-old sister over who gets the trike.

Children close in age quarrel more because they often find themselves in competition. For example, the twelve-year-old child will be less likely to see his seven-year-old sister as a competitive threat in a game of checkers and may even let her win the game to make her feel good. He will not, however, be so generous when playing checkers with his eleven-year-old sibling. In this situation, winning or losing becomes important because he subconsciously believes the game is a measure of his intelligence.

The problems presented by closely spaced children are not as bleak as they first appear. Although children close in age often quarrel more than children spaced further apart, when parents are careful to make sure that each child *feels* loved and special because of who he is and not because of what he can do in relation to his brothers and sisters, the quarreling behavior can be kept within tolerable limits. Also, closeness in age sometimes leads to emotional closeness later in life, as interests continue to mesh and competition dies down.

Age of Children as a Potential Factor Affecting Quarreling

Children under the age of two have more outbursts of anger which are not directed specifically toward another person. When angry, the toddler screams, cries, and throws toys. After the age of two, the child begins to direct his anger. Because siblings are sometimes nearby, the young child may direct his anger toward them. He expresses this anger in physical ways: taking toys from his sister, hitting her, knocking over her blocks. As children grow, their verbal skills increase and they learn to use language to express their anger. The physical expressions of their anger then become secondary.

When children enter the pre-teen years, there may be less sibling conflict simply because they are not together as much as when they were younger. They attend school during the day and play with friends outside the family after school. One child plays basketball while another attends a music lesson. Although the amount of fighting may be less among older children, the intensity of their quarrels often remains at the same level.

The New Baby and Sibling Rivalry

The arrival of a new baby is one of the most exciting events that can occur in a family. Eventually, however, the excitement settles and the reality of what this new child means to the family emerges. Each member of the family must, to some extent, rearrange his life to accommodate the newest addition to the family.

Mature parents accept the necessary rearrangement of their lives with relative ease. They take in stride the nights of interrupted sleep and the disappearance of leisure time.

For children, the acceptance of a new sibling is more difficult. They ask themselves: "Will I like having a baby around, or will a baby be a nuisance for me? Do Mommy and Daddy still love me, or do they love the baby more?"

Some children have a difficult time working out their confused feelings about the wrinkled "intruder" lying in the

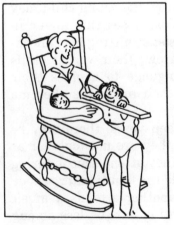

The New Baby and Sibling Rivalry

cradle, whom they both love and resent. The ease with which children adjust to a new sibling depends on a number of factors: age of the child, his position in the family (previously an only child or one of several children), his individual personality, and the way his parents act toward him and the new baby.

Age as a Factor Affecting Acceptance of a New Baby. Studies indicate that children between the ages of one and a half years to three years of age are likely to have more difficulty adjusting to a new brother or sister than a child who is older or one who is still an infant. Developmentally, this is easy to understand. Children from one and a half years to three years are self-centered and wish to possess and control everything and everyone around them. This is shown in their reluctance to share toys with others and in their striving to have their mother all to themselves. Feelings of security are fragile at this age. Anyone who interferes with this need to exclusively possess their mother, as a new baby does, is seen as an enemy and threat to their sense of security.

Children over the age of five usually have an easier time adjusting to a new sibling. In warm, caring homes, they have had more years to develop secure feelings about their identities and their relationships with their parents. They have had time to become secure in their parent's love for them. They are more independent and less likely to be disturbed when having to share their parents with a new sibling.

Children under the age of one and a half years also have an easier time accepting a new sibling. Children of this young age have not reached the maturity level in which they demand exclusive possession of a parent. They still need and want their mother's attention, but are not terrified at the thought of their parent attending to the needs of another child.

The age of a child when a new baby arrives *can* affect the ease with which he adjusts to a new sibling. However,

Difficulty Accepting a New Sibling

just because a child is between the age of one and a half years to three years of age does not mean he will have a difficult time making the adjustment. Many children of this age group adapt easily to the arrival of a new brother or sister. Likewise, some children in their teens have an extremely difficult time accepting a new sibling.

Dethroning of the Only Child and Sibling Rivalry. The child who has been an only child for a few years has some major adjustments to make when a new sibling appears. For example, three-year-old Corey is a delightful boy who is loved and cherished by his parents. Both sets of grandparents shower him with love and presents. Everyone enjoys being with Corey. Then Baby Kristi is born. Corey is no longer the center of attention. He has been dethroned.

At first, Corey is confused and doesn't understand what is happening to him. Before long, however, he realizes why he is no longer the center of attention—Baby Kristi. He much preferred being the only child, and understandably isn't terribly pleased with this new intruder who also receives love and attention from his parents and grandparents. His drop in status (as he sees it) causes him to feel angry and jealous.

Corey will need considerable help from his loving, sensitive parents to help him adjust to his new position in the family.

As with age, the position in the family that a child holds can be a potential factor affecting the ease with which a child adjusts to a new sibling. But its effect is minimal in comparison to other factors which we will now consider.

Personality Characteristics Affect Sibling Rivalry. The arrival of a baby presents a number of potential problems for the young child. The child is asked to adjust to a new, and for some children, frightening experience: accepting a new sibling who threatens his sense of security. Parents must, of necessity, take care of the infant's needs which means they must be "shared" by two children instead of possessed by one.

A child's individual personality is a major factor influencing the child's ability to accept and love a new brother or sister. Children whose personalities include strong feelings of security, who are "giving" in nature, who are independent, and who adapt easily to new experiences will have a minimum of difficulty accepting a new sibling. Conversely, children whose personalities include feelings of insecurity, who are extremely possessive, who are very dependent, and who have difficulty adapting to new experiences will have a more difficult time accepting and loving a new sibling. As these children grow older they will probably experience intense feelings of sibling rivalry which may result in bitter sibling conflicts.

Parent-Child Relationship as a Factor Affecting Sibling Rivalry. Perhaps the most important factor determining how easily the child adjusts to a new sibling is the way the parents handle the budding relationship between the child and the new baby. Parents who are sensitive, understanding, and accepting of the child's feelings about the new sibling can help their child sort out his confused feelings about his new position in the family. The child can be helped to realize that he is still very special and very much loved by his parents. This will greatly increase the chances of the child adjusting to and loving his new brother or sister.

Why Do Children Feel Jealous of a New Sibling?

It is common and normal for children to feel some jealousy toward a new sibling. The amount of jealousy children feel varies greatly. Some children experience only mild feelings of jealousy and are able to carry on with life not overly disturbed by the arrival of a new sibling. Other children, however, are extremely jealous of a new sibling and find it impossible to function normally as a result of those feelings.

When a new baby arrives on the scene, the older child looks the whole situation over carefully. If the child concludes that the new baby doesn't affect the amount of attention, approval, and love he receives from his parents, he will more readily accept and love the baby. If, however, the child concludes that his parents love him less because of the new baby, he will undoubtedly develop intense feelings of jealousy. Jealous children fear they are losing the love of their parents, a terrifying feeling for a child. Consider the following example:

Scotty is two years old and eagerly waits with his grandparents to see his new baby brother. His parents have told him how wonderful and cute this new baby will be, how much he will love him, and how much fun it will be for Scotty to have someone to play with.

Scotty knows the big event must be important because Daddy bought a big cake to celebrate, Grandpa brought his camera to take pictures, and Grandma worked a long time knitting a sweater for the baby.

Scotty watches as everyone rushes out the door toward the car, smiling, and pushing to hold Baby Benjamin. A lot of people come to visit, bringing presents for the baby and saying how wonderful he is. Some tell Scotty how lucky he is to have a new baby brother.

Scotty isn't so sure. He thinks, maybe, things were better when everyone brought him presents and smiled and were happy to be with him.

Scotty is confused. Subconsciously, he wonders, "Do Mommy and Daddy still love me or do they love Benjamin more than me because he is little? Do I love Benjamin? Should I love Benjamin? Is he going to cause problems for me? Will Mommy and Daddy love me less because they have to give some love to Benjamin?"

All children, including Scotty, will feel some degree of insecurity at the birth of a new baby. Whether these insecure feelings lessen with time, or grow into major emotional problems depends on how the child answers that important question: Do Mommy and Daddy love me less now that they have a new baby?

Obviously, we can never know for sure what is going through Scotty's mind, but we can imagine what Scotty might be thinking as he tries to answer those important questions, which are illustrated on page 26.

SUMMARY OF FACTORS AFFECTING SIBLING RIVALRY AND QUARRELING

There is a *tendency* for siblings to quarrel more when they are of the same sex, when they are spaced close in age, when they are younger, and when their position in the family (i.e. oldest child, middle child) causes them to feel less loved than their siblings. It is important to emphasize the word "tendency" because these findings are not hard and fast rules. One can easily find children closely spaced in age, of the same sex, who have warm, caring relationships with each other and a minimum of quarreling in their homes. Likewise,

SCOTTY WONDERS:	SCOTTY LOOKS THE SITUATION OVER AND COLLECTS EVIDENCE:	SCOTTY CONCLUDES:
1. "Do Mommy and Daddy love the new baby?"	"They kiss him. They look happy when they hold him. They tell other people how wonderful he is." →	"Mommy and Daddy love the baby."
2. "Do Mommy and Daddy still love me?"	"They kiss and hug me. Daddy still gives me piggyback rides. Mommy brought me a truck when she came home from the hospital."	"Of course, Mommy and Daddy still love me."
	or	
	"Daddy said he was too tired to play with me, but he played with the baby. They kiss me fast when I go to bed, and then they rock that baby for a long time." →	"I'm not sure. Maybe Mommy and Daddy don't love me any more."
3. "Do Mommy and Daddy love me less now that Baby Benjamin is here?"	"Mommy hugs me and says, 'I love you Scotty. You are so wonderful.' She says she really likes boys that are three-years-old. She says I am helpful to her when I hand her baby powder and put Benjamin's pacifier back in. Daddy smiles and says, 'Let's go for a walk together, Scott. Just you and me.'" →	"Mommy and Daddy sure love me a lot. They love me just as much as they did before Baby Benjamin came."
	or	
	"Mommy says, 'You have to feed yourself now because I must feed the baby.' Daddy brought Baby Benjamin a soft Teddy Bear. He didn't bring me anything. They don't rock me any more but they do Benjamin. They say I am too big for that." →	"I don't think Mommy and Daddy love me as much as they used to. And it's all because of Baby Benjamin."

there are families with children of opposite sexes spaced many years apart who feel very hostile toward each other and fight continually.

Another factor which affects sibling relationships is the birth of a new sibling. When a new baby is introduced into the family, his siblings carefully observe how their parents act toward the infant and toward them. If older siblings view the new baby as competition for their parents' love and affection, jealous feelings are sure to develop and sibling rivalry will be off to a running start.

However, the home environment moderates these factors. Children whose parents help them feel good about themselves and comfortable in the position they have in the family are much more likely to develop caring, sharing, and helping relationships with their siblings. Their sibling relationships will be less affected by their age, sex, position in the family, or the arrival of a new baby.

ARE MY CHILDREN JEALOUS OF EACH OTHER?

The child who believes that his parents love him less than a younger or older sibling is terrified. He struggles to find ways to gain his parents' approval and love. Children express their jealous feelings toward their siblings in a number of ways depending on their age and personality.

Jealousy Expressed by the Young Child

The young child may express his jealousy toward siblings by engaging in babylike behaviors. He whines or cries easily over daily situations. He clings to a parent, afraid to venture off in play with neighborhood children. He is reluctant to attend nursery school, wanting instead to stay home with Mommy. His speech may be babyish.

If the jealousy is toward a new baby, the young child may resort to regressive behavior. Although toilet trained for some time, he has frequent accidents. The child may get into the baby's crib which previously belonged to him or he may express a desire to nurse or suck on a bottle. These behaviors may or may not be signs of jealousy. It is possible that the child wants to get into the crib and nurse simply because he is curious to know what it feels like. It is his way of finding out what it is like to be a baby. If, however, these behaviors continue for a period of time, they may actually be symptoms of his jealousy toward the new baby. Such regressive behaviors may indicate that the child feels insecure since the arrival of his new sibling. He wants more attention and subconsciously decides the way to get that attention is to be like a baby: "Adults give babies a lot of attention. I want attention, so I'll act like a baby."

Jealousy is sometimes expressed by children in aggressive ways: getting into a sibling's prized possessions, intentionally breaking a sibling's toy, biting his brother, or grabbing toys from his sister.

Jealousy Expressed in Misbehavior

Jealousy Expressed through
Sibling Quarrels

One of the most common expressions of sibling jealousy is quarreling. This is easy to understand. The child who feels he must struggle for his "fair share" of parental love will undoubtedly have hostile feelings toward his sibling, with whom he must compete. Often, he will tease, antagonize, and degrade his sibling's personal character. Unconsciously, the jealous child chooses ways to behave which will attract his parents' attention, and fighting among brothers and sisters usually does attract parents' attention.

Subtle Expressions of
Jealousy

Some parents believe it reflects badly on them when their children show signs of sibling rivalry, thus they try to root out all *signs* of rivalry among their children. Children in such families try to hide their jealousy of a sibling because they know their parents do not approve of such feelings.

Although it is possible for parents to get rid of most open signs of sibling rivalry, the jealous feelings remain. Eventually, these jealous feelings appear in behaviors which are more destructive than simple, open expressions of rivalry. For example, the child may express jealousy by becoming overly "good." He kisses, hugs, and runs to meet his younger sibling's every whimper. Or he rushes to comply to all his older sibling's demands. Parents may mistakenly interpret this overly "good" behavior as an abundance of sibling love, when in fact the child acts this way in order to win his parents' approval. He is desperately seeking love and approval and believes his parents like children who are "good." The child works hard to always look good in his parents' eyes.

This kind of approval, however, is not a sufficient substitute for genuine love of the child.

Subtle Expression of Jealousy

Other subtle expressions of jealousy include: nightmares, excessive competitiveness, meekness, stuttering, tics, excessive shyness, and excessive generosity.

Subtle expressions of jealousy are less obvious and *may appear* less troublesome, however, they are clear evidence that a child is feeling less loved by his parents. It is important for parents to notice these less conspicuous signs of jealousy and help the child deal with his jealous feelings.

HELPING CHILDREN DEAL WITH JEALOUSY

Encourage Children to Express Their Feelings about Siblings. The first step we can take in helping children deal with their jealous feelings is to admit that those feelings probably do exist, to a lesser or greater degree. Next, we must allow and encourage our children to express their feelings openly, assuring them that we will not judge or criticize those feelings.

We need, also, to listen with an empathetic ear and try to understand why they feel the way they do.

By encouraging children to express their feelings about their siblings, we give them and ourselves the opportunity to learn how they may have acquired jealous feelings. We may find that some of the children's jealousy has developed because they have misinterpreted some of our words and actions to mean that we love their siblings more than we love them. In most cases, parents do not favor one sibling over another. However, the child may think his parents love his siblings more because he misinterprets his parents' words and actions. For example:

SITUATION:	CHILD MISINTERPRETS:	CHILD CONCLUDES:
Susan has outgrown a perfectly good coat. Since it fits Jenny, she inherits the coat.	"Susan always gets → new clothes, I always get the old things."	"Mother loves Susan → more than me."
Daddy is happy to have a new son and → enjoys playing with him.	"Daddy talks all the time about the baby. → He doesn't get that excited about me."	"Daddy loves the baby more than me because he is a boy and I am a girl."
Mother tells Jill how much she → enjoys listening to her play the piano.	Jill's sister thinks: → "Jill is better in music than I am."	"I'm not good in → music. I'm not very good at things."

Does this mean parents should never pass clothing on to a younger child? Should we hide our excitement over having a new son? Must we suppress our pleasure at seeing one child play the piano well? Should we compliment each child in secret for fear his sibling might know of our positive feelings

toward him? Of course not. Expressing positive feelings
toward children helps them to feel loved.

What we must remember, however, is that when we give
warm, positive messages to one child, we are also giving
messages to the other child. We must be sensitive to what
those messages might say to the observing child. Children
are less likely to misinterpret positive messages given to
their siblings if they themselves feel secure in their parents'
love. Children whose need for parental love is being fulfilled
develop a minimum of jealousy toward their siblings and
experience much less sibling rivalry and quarreling.

Preparing Young Children for the Arrival of a New Sibling

The beginnings of intense sibling rivalry can often be
traced back to the first few weeks and months after the birth
of a new sibling. The child who feels insecure about his
parents' love has a difficult time accepting and loving a new
sibling. When the child sees his parents loving the new baby,
he becomes even more insecure about his parents' love. The
insecure child finds it difficult to share parental love because
he feels there is already not enough to go around.

If, instead, the child receives as much love as he needs
and desires *before* the baby arrives, the child is less concerned
about a new sibling also receiving love from his parents. He
feels secure that there is enough parental love for both of
them.

The child is less confused over the birth of a new brother
or sister if parents take time to prepare him for this new
experience. One way to introduce children to what babies are
like is to show them their own baby books. Even older
children enjoy looking at their baby books as you tell them
what they were like as babies. Children of all ages like to
hear how much they were loved as babies, how cute they

were as three-year-olds, and how much you enjoy and love them right now, whatever age they are.

Linda sits on her mother's lap and listens intently as her mother leafs through her baby book:

> *Linda, this is a picture of Daddy holding you when we were still at the hospital. Look how cute you are. The nurses wanted to hold you all the time, but we said, "She's our special baby girl and we must take her home with us." Grandpa took this picture of you when you were sleeping. You are wearing the sweater Grandma made for you. Here you are walking for the first time. Remember when you put your hand in the cake when you were two? And now you are four years old. You go to nursery school. I surely am glad you are four years old. You are a wonderful girl.*

This mother is helping her child realize that she was loved when she was a baby and is very much loved now that she is four years old.

Children should be told ahead of time that they will have a new baby brother or sister so they can take part in preparing for the new baby. They feel included in this special event when they select nightgowns and bibs or contribute some of their own belongings, such as a stuffed animal or baby brush, to the new baby.

For the very young child, Mother's sudden disappearance on delivery day can be frightening. It is difficult for the child to understand why his mother has left him so abruptly and stayed away so long. Parents can help their child prepare for the eventual, sudden disappearance of their mother. For example, a few weeks before their baby was due, one mother asked her son, Sean, to sit with her while she drew some pictures. She first drew a picture of a rather "chubby" lady packing a suitcase. She explained to Sean that the lady is Mommy and she is packing a suitcase because she will need to leave home a few days while the baby is born. Next, she drew a picture of Aunt Lou, the family dog, and Sean waving goodbye to Mommy and Daddy leaving in the car. The series of pictures continued; with mother resting in a hospital bed with the new baby; Aunt Lou, at home eating with Sean; Daddy, Mommy, and baby coming home; and Mommy and Daddy hugging Sean while Aunt Lou held the baby. The drawings took several days to complete, each session being a time when Sean and his mother talked about what was going to happen. Gradually, Sean began to understand that his mother would leave quickly and stay away for a few days while his favorite Aunt Lou took care of him. Also, he understood that soon his whole family would be back together again and his Mommy and Daddy would hug and love Sean very much.

The young child can better visualize what will be happening on that special day when his mother quickly leaves if his parents take him on a trial trip to the hospital. He will thoroughly enjoy lugging Mommy's empty suitcase into the car, driving the route to the hospital, and seeing the big hospital where his mother will stay for a few days.

Getting Off to a Good Start

The first few days with the new baby are most important in helping the young child accept his new sibling and feel secure that he is loved by his parents. Parents should not assume, "Of course we still love our child. He knows that." This thought may be true and very clear in the parents' minds, but the child needs to be reassured of it.

We help children feel loved by spending time with them. During that time together, children need to know that they are special to us, that they bring us joy, that we care very much about them, and that they are huggable, kissable, and lovable. Children need to know that others their age are nice to be with.

One mistake made by some parents in their attempt to make the older child feel loved, is to say negative things about the new baby, such as, "Your new sister cries all the time, and can't do the things you can." Statements of this kind do not strengthen the child's feelings of being loved. The child may temporarily like the comparison in which he shines, but soon the child realizes that his parents compare the two of them and that he may not always come out on top. Even at this young age, making comparisons between children is a sure way to plant the seeds of jealousy among siblings which can grow and choke out the possibilities of warm, loving, sibling relationships.

chapter 3

Pressure from Parents, Teachers, Peers

Pressure from Parents

It is natural for parents to want their children to do well in school, keep their room neat, eat nutritious foods, get along well with others, be skillful in sports, keep their fingernails clean, and so on. We feel it is our responsibility as parents to help our children attain certain goals. However, sometimes we aren't too sure how best to accomplish this and resort to pressuring our children through nagging, pushing, scolding, shaming, blaming, warning, threatening, and punishing.

For example, Stuart's parents felt he had academic ability and wanted their son to get better grades in school. They reminded Stuart continuously of their desire for him to do better with such pressuring techniques as:

PUNISHING: O.K. your grades are not what we wanted, so there will be no friends over until you show us you can do better.

NAGGING: Don't dawdle so long at dinner. Remember, you have homework to do.

SHAMING: You should be embarrassed to bring home a report card like that.

WARNING: You will be sorry when all your friends go off to college, and you can't even get in.

It is very unlikely that Stuart will improve his grades due to his parents' pressuring techniques. Instead, his parents will probably make Stuart frustrated, angry, and perhaps hostile. In addition to worrying about his grades, Stuart must now deal with his accumulated feelings of frustration and anger.

Stuart may keep his anger to himself, or he may choose to vent his anger openly. Although Stuart is most angry at his parents for the unfair way he feels they have treated him, he probably will not show his anger to them. Very possibly,

Parental Pressure Causing Sibling Quarrel

Stuart will take his anger out on his brothers and sisters. When parents criticize, scold, shame, and blame their children, those children often use the same techniques on their siblings, resulting in an increase in sibling conflicts. Children do need our *guidance* and *encouragement* to accomplish desired goals but they do not need our *pressure*. Pressure applied to children only causes additional problems and often results in deteriorating sibling relationships.

Pressure from Teachers

Teachers naturally expect children to excel in school. However, when teachers expect all children to excel at the same rate, and have unrealistic expectations for some children in their classrooms, they may begin to apply excessive amounts of pressure on children to perform. This causes those children to feel incompetent, insecure, and disliked by the teacher.

I am always amazed and saddened to walk into a classroom and find 25 children staring at the same page in a math book. Just as certainly as there are some students among the 25 who are bored with the simple lesson, there are some children who feel great pressure to learn the material which they are not yet capable of grasping.

Pressure to excel is evident in charts offering stars only to children who have mastered certain skills and in displays of the "best" papers on walls. Teachers who pressure children with unrealistic expectations make them feel stupid and frustrated. The children are angry at their teacher for asking too much of them, for broadcasting their lack of achievement and for labeling them as incompetent. They may also be angry with themselves for not achieving like other children.

The child who is not doing well in school, or more importantly, thinks he is not doing well, takes his negative feelings, pressures, and frustrations home with him. He carries a limp banana peel home in his lunch box and his limp feelings of worthlessness home in his heart.

One way children deal with their frustrations is to take them out on their brothers and sisters, thus increasing quarreling among siblings. For example, a junior high teacher of English did not like boys. She found them to be rude, irresponsible, and trouble in her class. This attitude carried over in her grading practices: rarely did a boy receive an A in her class.

Tony was a boy who had always done well in English but in her class, no matter how hard he tried, he could not attain the mark he felt he deserved. Tony was frustrated by his inability to communicate with this teacher.

Tony brought his feelings of frustration and anger home with him. He became much more argumentative in his relationships with his sisters. His past kind and playful behavior toward his sisters disappeared.

When Tony's parents recognized what his teacher's attitude was doing to him, they requested that he be changed to another class. His grades improved and there was an immediate improvement in Tony's relationships with his sisters.

When teachers place unnecessary pressure on children, causing them to feel frustrated and angry, the resulting feelings are often vented on siblings.

Peer Pressure

Soon after entering school, children begin to want to be like their friends, or peers. It becomes very important to them to dress, talk, and act like other children. They may feel great pressure to conform to what their peers are doing. For example, one seven-year-old girl came home crying to her mother, "I told the kids I didn't have any red-striped socks, but they said, 'If you don't wear red-striped socks, you're out.' " It was very important for this child to belong to her peer group and she was devastated at the thought of being excluded.

Children of all ages feel some pressure to conform to peer group expectations. For some children, however, this pressure is accentuated by the fact that they do not possess the skills to allow them to conform to peer group expectations. These children are made to feel 'out of it' by their peers.

I recall a fourth grade boy, Ryan, who suffered rejection because of his lack of athletic ability. Every recess the boys gathered to play kickball. Two team captains chose their players, the most skillful players being chosen first. Ryan was the least skillful of all and was chosen last, if at all. Ryan felt rejected by his peers and thought of himself as inadequate.

The rejection was dramatically apparent when someone told the teacher a child had gone out of the schoolyard to gather hickory nuts from the neighboring yard. She asked the class who had trespassed on personal property. The children looked around, and one finally said, "It was Ryan." Ryan was not guilty and denied the act. Unwisely, the teacher had the class decide who was telling the truth. She asked, "Who saw Ryan cross onto private property?" Almost unanimously, the class members raised their hands.

Ryan was rejected by nearly all his peers. He felt sad, frustrated, and angry. He did not show his anger toward his peers, knowing this would cause him further painful rejection, but took the frustration home with him and released it on his younger brother. He told his brother he wouldn't play catch with "a baby." Ryan teased and goaded his brother as his classmates had done to him at school.

Pressure from parents to achieve, pressure from teachers to perform, and pressure from peers to conform can cause children to feel frustrated and angry. These angry feelings often find expression in hostile sibling conflicts.

chapter 4

Home Atmosphere

The emotional tone found in the home strongly affects the quality of sibling relationships. In a study of anger in young children, Florence Goodenough notes:

> *"A major factor determining the frequency with which anger is displayed by children is to be found in the intangible relationships existing between the members of the household—the so-called "home atmosphere." (Goodenough, 1931, p. 243)*

In families where the general home atmosphere is positive, warm, and supportive, there will be less sibling conflict. In contrast, a negative, critical, and hostile home atmosphere will encourage high levels of sibling conflict.

CHARACTERISTICS OF THE
POSITIVE AND NEGATIVE HOME
ATMOSPHERE

Listed below are some of the characteristics found in families with positive and negative home atmospheres. Certainly, no family will exhibit all the characteristics of either of these extremes at all times. Rather, most families' homes will be found somewhere between these two extremes. The family home atmosphere will also vary from day to day, some days being more positive than others.

POSITIVE HOME ATMOSPHERE	NEGATIVE HOME ATMOSPHERE
enthusiasm	destructive expressions of anger
caring	lack of enthusiasm
sharing	rigid thinking
warmth	negative attitudes
cooperation	put-downs
supportive interactions	floundering, searching behaviors
positive attitudes	criticism of others
acceptance of others	hostility
purposeful behaviors	rejection of others
patience	defeated attitudes
empathy	apathy
expressions of joy	demanding, nagging, blaming
focus on the positive aspects of life	focus on the negative aspects of life

A positive home atmosphere allows and encourages children to develop positive feelings about themselves. Children who possess positive feelings about themselves are more inclined to have positive feelings about others, and are better able to develop warm, loving sibling relationships.

The negative home atmosphere is conducive to the development of negative feelings about the self in children.

Children who feel badly about themselves are more likely to have difficulty accepting and loving others, and are more inclined to have difficulty getting along with their brothers and sisters.

WHAT DETERMINES THE QUALITY OF THE HOME ATMOSPHERE?

Every member of the family contributes to some extent to the overall quality of the home atmosphere. However, parents generally have the greatest influence, and they set the stage for initiating and encouraging a positive or negative home atmosphere. One perceptive parent notes the influence she has on the home atmosphere of her family:

> *The home atmosphere in our family seems to change from one day to the next. Some days we all act civil to each other and get along well, while other days are disasters. It does seem we have better days when I start the morning off on a positive note. But, if I wake up in a bad mood and grump at the kids, they soon begin grumping at each other. It's like a chain reaction and I am often the one who starts it. Actually, my husband starts it. If he kisses me when he leaves for work and says, "Have a good day, honey," the whole family is in for a better day, and the home atmosphere is definitely more positive.*

IMPROVING THE HOME ATMOSPHERE

Improving the home atmosphere requires the participation and effort of all family members, especially the parents. Parents can set the stage for improving the home atmosphere by conscientiously being more positive in their relationships with family members. Setting such an example for the family will spread positive feelings throughout the family, just as a stone tossed in a still pond causes one ripple which in turn sets off a second ripple, then the third, and so on. Kind words, understanding looks, and helpful actions will spread from the parents to other family members and back again, each reinforcing the last and encouraging the next.

Behaving in more positive ways toward others is not always easy. It is especially difficult when we are faced with personal problems: pending divorce, financial worries, emotional difficulties, job problems. When greatly troubled, a person will not have the energy or focus to work on creating a positive home atmosphere.

Most parents, however, are able through their own efforts to improve the quality of the home atmosphere. One way in which family members can actively improve the home atmosphere is to be more positive toward and accepting of all members of the family, thus making them feel more worthwhile and lovable.

Even the youngest child in the family can work toward improving the home atmosphere as did one six-year-old. Jenny came home from kindergarten telling her mother about "warm fuzzies" and "cold pricklies." Jenny explained, "A warm fuzzy is when you say, 'I like your hat' or 'I'm sorry that you're sick.' A cold pricklie is when you say, 'I don't like

Spreading Of Positive Feelings

your hair' or 'You do dumb work.' If someone gives you a warm fuzzy, it makes you feel good and happy. When someone gives you a cold pricklie, it makes you feel sad and mad. Do you want a warm fuzzy, Mommy?" Jenny hugs her mother saying, "I love you, Mommy."

Jenny's warm fuzzy made her mother feel good and happier the rest of the day. She felt like giving out more warm fuzzies to her husband and son later that evening. They were somewhat puzzled by her showering of warmth and affection, but each liked the warm fuzzies, felt better, and also became more positive toward family members. That evening the home atmosphere was warm and supportive, with everyone feeling good about themselves and the other family members.

If enough sincere, warm fuzzies are passed among family members, the home-tone improves. Brothers and sisters who learn to give and receive warm fuzzies will have less time for hostile, damaging sibling conflicts.

TIME TO GROW CLOSE

The development of a positive home atmosphere requires that family members know each other well, care about each other, and spend time expressing feelings to each other. It is not enough to quickly say, "I love you," It takes time for families to grow close and communicate love to one another.

Unfortunately, some families have difficulty finding the necessary time to nurture positive family relationships. After job obligations, schoolwork, and home chores are completed, other activities compete for the "free time." Two major competitors for free time are: 1) extracurricular activities; and 2) the family television.

Extracurricular Activities. Members of a family may engage in many desirable outside activities which bring pleasure to their lives: church choir, Campfire Girls, Boy Scouts, PTA meetings, bowling leagues, parties, concerts, and so on. However, an overabundance of such desirable activities leaves little time for family members to spend together. The children and parents of such a busy family *pass* each other many times a day on their way to varied activities, but all too often, they do not *touch* one another. Such a flurry of activities, no matter how desirable, can keep family members from sufficient interaction.

The Family T.V.   Television also competes for parents' and children's free time. In many households, television wins at the expense of family members spending quality time together. It is not enough that parents and children share the sofa while viewing hours of television. They must share their lives with each other.

The development of a positive home atmosphere requires that family members take time to grow close—time devoted to listening, caring, sharing, supporting, or, in other words, loving one another.

chapter 5

Physical Causes of Quarreling

LACK OF SLEEP

The kind of quarrel we hear late at night in the car coming home from Grandma's house often occurs because the children are tired. Not surprisingly, studies on the relationship between lack of sleep and irritability unquestionably support the idea that children quarrel more when they are tired (Neisser, 1951). Fortunately, there is a quick cure for quarrels caused by lack of sleep. Making sure children get to bed earlier so they can get enough sleep will eliminate quarrels caused by fatigue.

What is "enough" sleep for a child? The answer depends on the age of the child and his personal body requirements for sleep. One four-year-old may require eleven hours of sleep

Children Quarrel More When They Are Tired

at night and a two-hour nap in the afternoon, while another four-year-old functions perfectly well on eleven hours of sleep at night and no afternoon nap. The following information indicates the average amount of sleep per day for children of different ages (Goodenough, 1931).

1-6 months	15 hours
6-12 months	14 hours
1-1½ years	13½ hours
1½-2 years	13 hours
2-3 years	12¾ hours
3-4 years	12 hours
5-6 years	11¾ hours
6-7 years	11 hours

This sleep information can indicate to us if our child is departing drastically from the average amount of sleep found for children of his age. However, it does not allow for individual differences in sleep requirements and we should not expect our child to sleep exactly the number of hours listed. Perhaps the best guide to how much sleep a child requires is ~ur observation of how quickly he falls asleep after going to bed and how tired he appears to be during his waking hours. One mother received the clue from her five-year-old daughter that she no longer needed an afternoon nap when the child confided to her, "I didn't really sleep, Mommy, 'cause my head was too full of thinking."

HUNGER

Another observation which is not surprising to any parent who has tried to prepare dinner while attending to hungry children is that children fight more when they are hungry (Neisser, 1951). Research supports this observation. The three-year-old boy who explains his attack on his brother with, "I bit my brother 'cause I'm hungry" is probably quite accurate in his assessment of the motive behind his behavior.

Knowing that children often quarrel more when they are hungry supports the popular idea that a full stomach makes for contentment. This being the case, one strategy is to offer children a light, nutritious snack mid-morning and mid-afternoon.

Children Quarrel More When They Are Hungry

ILLNESS

It has been found that children with minor illnesses quarrel more (Neisser, 1951). We can easily understand this, for as adults we also are inclined to be more irritable when we have mild colds, slight digestive disturbances, constipation, and so on.

Children who have more serious health problems are less likely to quarrel with their siblings. Two reasons for this have been suggested: 1) seriously ill children are too sick to engage in outbursts toward a sibling, and 2) parents concerned over the seriousness of their child's illness may give the child more attention and instruct other children in the family to be extra nice to them because they are sick.

Fatigue, hunger and minor illness quarrels, while annoying, are not rooted in deep underlying emotional difficulties and do not result in serious, long-term damage to children. Curing such quarrels is relatively simple: remove the physical cause and the quarrels disappear.

chapter 6

Inability to Express Anger Constructively

Ten-year-old Chris has a coin collection which he displays in neat blue booklets on his shelf in his bedroom. Five-year-old Marcia has a friend over to play grocery store. Needing "real" money to play store, Marcia remembers the pennies in Chris' room.

When Chris comes home from school he finds all his pennies punched out of the blue booklets. He is furious.

It is easy to understand why Chris is terribly angry at his sister when he finds his coin collection demolished. What will Chris do next? How will he express the anger he feels? In a similar situation, how would one of your children express his anger? Would he respond in one of the following ways?

Verbal Attack   Getting Back   Physical Attack

Hidden Anger   Constructive Expression of Anger

CHILDREN EXPRESS ANGER IN DIFFERENT WAYS

All children get angry over things that happen to them in their everyday lives. They become angry when brothers take their bikes without permission, when sisters change their T.V. programs, and when their siblings won't share the cookies in the jar.

However, the *ways* in which children express their anger vary from one child to another. Some children attempt to hide their anger, although it often surfaces in other forms, such as extreme shyness, compulsive eating, nervous disorders, tics, stomach ulcers, and extreme competitiveness.

Some children show anger physically. They might bite their brothers, yell at their mothers, slug their sisters, break toys, throw tantrums, slam doors, or kick the cat.

Other children express anger verbally. They attack another person (often their siblings) with words, degrading their personal character with such labels as "dumb," "lazy," and "mean."

Some children get right to the point of their anger. In other words, they inform the offender *why* they are angry: "I am really angry because you ruined my coin collection. Now I have to fix it. You made me waste a lot of time. Don't get into my coins ever again."

Why do some children hit, some sulk, some swear, and others "tell it like it is" when they become angry? Probably because of the different ways they have seen anger expressed in their homes.

CHILDREN "LEARN" WAYS TO EXPRESS THEIR ANGER

Children, as we know, are great imitators. The infant imitates his mother's clapping hands. The toddler watches his older sibling and tries to copy the way he climbs stairs, two at a time. The preschool child pretends to shave like Daddy.

Children of all ages watch how people around them act. They "try on" some of the behaviors they see. If those behaviors feel comfortable and get desired results, they become part of the child. If the behaviors are not comfortable, the child discards them and tries new ones.

Parents are usually the strongest role models for children. It is sometimes frightening to think our children continually watch us and copy our personal behaviors. No matter how hard we try to get out of the spotlight by lecturing "Do what I say, not what I do," the child will probably do what we do and not what we say.

In addition to many other behaviors, children carefully watch what people do when they get angry. Children learn to express their own anger by imitating the way they see people near them expressing their anger. Evidence indicates that children who are punished through physical means—spanking, jerking, slapping—are much more likely to be physical when they themselves become angry (Mussen, 1977). Consider the case in which the angry father paddles his young child yelling, "I hope this paddling teaches you a lesson. You can't go around hitting your sister just because you are mad at her." The child is certainly being taught a lesson loud and clear: when people get mad at someone, they express their anger by hitting. Thus, when the child becomes angry at his sister again he hits her.

Some parents express their anger through verbally beating the people around them. Mother is angry at her teenage son because he failed to take out the morning garbage. She expresses her anger by providing a verbal beating of her son: "You are good-for-nothing, forgetful, and lazy." The child watches his angry mother and how she expresses anger. He concludes: "If you get mad at someone, tear them apart verbally." This child will probably verbally tear apart his brothers and sisters when he becomes angry at them, thus fueling bitter sibling quarrels.

Research supports the idea that children imitate their parents' methods of dealing with anger. Children who use antisocial aggression and assaultive behavior tend much more frequently to come from families where there are parents who act as aggressive models (Lefkowitz, 1977).

DOES THIS MEAN I SHOULD NEVER GET ANGRY AT MY CHILDREN?

Of course not. All parents get angry at their children. It is not harmful to children to know that you are angry and that your anger has to do with their behavior. The harm does not come from the anger itself, but rather, from how the parent expresses that anger. It is harmful to children when parents express their anger through abusive physical or verbal attacks. Children often imitate these destructive expressions of anger with their siblings.

Parental anger can be expressed in constructive ways which do not hurt children. Civilized expressions of anger become desirable models for children to copy. When children see their parents express anger in constructive, civil ways, they are more likely to express their own anger in similar ways.

WHAT ARE CONSTRUCTIVE EXPRESSIONS OF ANGER?

Let's look at an example: Ten-year-old Elizabeth and her friend were given permission to walk home after school and stop for an ice cream cone on the way. The trip home, allowing for the treat, should have taken 30–40 minutes. When an hour had passed, Elizabeth's mother nervously glanced at the clock. She called the school and ice cream store and found that the girls had left long ago. All kinds of frightening thoughts entered her mind. She drove along their path, looking for the girls with no success. Returning home, she finds the girls laughing and having a good time on the front steps. Realizing they are safe, her fear turns to anger.

Elizabeth's mother is angry because her daughter did

not come directly home after the ice cream treat as she was
told to do. She expresses her anger in a constructive manner:

MOTHER: Elizabeth, you were to stop for ice cream and then
come directly home. It has been two hours since
school was dismissed. Where have you been?

ELIZABETH: We stopped at the cemetery on the way home. We
were looking at all the people and when they died.
I didn't know it was so late.

MOTHER: Do you realize how worried I was? When you didn't
arrive home I thought something might have happened to you.

ELIZABETH: I'm sorry, Mother.

MOTHER: I'm sure it must have been interesting to look at
tombstones, but you should have told me where
you planned to go so I would not worry.

This mother's anger was caused by the fear she felt over
her daughter's safety. She expressed her anger openly but in
a constructive manner:

1. She told Elizabeth *why* she was angry—"because your
behavior (not telling me where you were) caused me to
worry."
2. She told Elizabeth what was wrong with her behavior—"You were to come directly home after ice cream.
You did not."
3. She gave Elizabeth important information about what
is desirable behavior—"Tell me your plans ahead of
time."

Notice that Elizabeth's mother is not disapproving of
Elizabeth herself, calling her irresponsible, forgetful, or

sneaky. She disapproves only of her behavior in this one incidence. Elizabeth can continue her day knowing she made a mistake, but that her mother still loves her just as much. Anger has been expressed *constructively* by this mother.

Constructive expressions of anger focus on the behavior rather than on the worth of the person. Enraged expressions of anger toward the child himself distracts the child's attention away from *what* is being said to *how* it is being said. The child is so afraid of being swatted across the mouth or verbally destroyed that he does not have energy left to think about what is being said to him.

If children observe their parents expressing anger in nonconstructive ways, they probably will imitate such behaviors, and have loud, enraged conflicts with their brothers and sisters. They will spend so much time yelling and hitting each other they will not be able to focus on the real problem. We must help children learn to focus on the reasons for their anger and learn to express that anger in constructive ways. Children can best learn this by imitating parents who use constructive methods of dealing with their own anger.

SIBLINGS, PEERS, AND OTHERS AS MODELS

Parents are the primary and most significant models of behavior which children observe and imitate, but they are not the only models available to children. Brothers and sisters, school friends, and other adults in the child's life also influence behavior as models.

Older brothers and sisters act as models for younger children in the family. If older children express anger through physical and verbal abuse, the younger children may follow such behavior. This is particularly true when parents are absent a great deal from their children's lives.

School friends influence children's behavior also. This is

especially true as children grow older and peer acceptance and pressure exert a powerful influence on their behavior. Children want to be like their friends and will copy the peer group's accepted behaviors. If the peer group uses physical and verbal abuse to communicate, the vulnerable youngster may imitate such behavior.

DOES WATCHING VIOLENCE ON TELEVISION AFFECT HOW MY CHILDREN HANDLE THEIR ANGER?

Based on Nielsen Index figures, Michael Rothenberg states that: "The average American child will have viewed some 15,000 hours of television by the time he has completed high school" (Rothenberg, 1980). During those hours in front of the television he is exposed to numerous acts of violence, including stabbings, beatings, stompings, muggings, and less graphic but equally destructive forms of cruelty. He is often given destructive examples of how adults handle their anger.

The question parents often ask is, "Does watching violent television programs have any real effect on my child, since he knows they are only acting?" Research indicates that, yes, television violence influences children's behavior. Characters on TV serve as models which are imitated by some children:

> *Numerous studies clearly and uniformly confirm that the effects of television are extremely forceful and that television characters are taken as models; children imitate the aggressive behaviors they witness on the television screen. There is indisputable evidence that aggressive behaviors are directly acquired from television programs and retained. Children become more aggressive in behavior and attitudes following exposure to television violence, and these effects are both immediate and long-term. Violence on television, even cartoon violence, may also*

have negative effects on children's prosocial responses, reducing cooperation and sharing with peers (Lefkowitz, 1977, p. 103).

The implications of such research findings are self-evident. Children do imitate the people they see on television. If the child tries on behaviors he sees on TV and those behaviors fit comfortably, the child will adopt them. Parents should monitor the viewing habits of their children. If parents are strong, positive models of behaviors and children do not watch an excess of TV violence, the effects of TV modeling may be minimal. If, however, television is the strongest and most visible model, children will imitate and adopt the behaviors of the characters they view on television. In such cases, television will have strong, negative effects on the child's behavior.

Children who are surrounded with models who express anger in hostile, aggressive ways will express their own anger toward their brothers and sisters in a similar manner:

. . . the more a child is exposed to aggressive behavior in others, in real life or on television, the more likely he is to manifest such behavior himself and incorporate aggressive behavior as part of his self-concept (Hamacheck, 1971, p. 151).

CHILDREN "TRY ON" BEHAVIORS

Even parents who provide desirable models for their children to imitate cannot be certain that they will learn healthy ways to express anger, as this example illustrates:

Craig is an eight-year-old boy who has not been allowed to watch any television program more violent than "Captain Kangaroo." His parents would never think of spanking Craig. Yet, Craig is one of the most physically aggressive children in the neighborhood.

With such strong, desirable models for him to imitate, why does Craig express his anger in physically aggressive ways such as throwing his bat when he strikes out and initiating numerous fights with his peers and siblings?

We noted earlier that children "try on" many kinds of behavior. Those behaviors which fit comfortably, the child adopts as his own. Parents, to a great extent, determine whether the child will feel comfortable in certain behaviors. Craig has tried on physically aggressive behaviors and has found that they fit quite well and work for him. For example, in one encounter with his mother, Craig was angry because she insisted he wear a hat on a cold, winter morning. Craig expressed his anger by picking up a toy and throwing it across the room. For fear of suppressing Craig's anger, his mother ignored the behavior and said nothing as Craig walked out the door without his hat.

Craig "tried on" the behavior of throwing things when angry and it fit comfortably. His aggressive display of anger allowed him to get his way in not wearing a hat. Because his physical display of anger worked for him in this instance, he is likely to use the same behavior in the future when he is angry.

Should Children Settle Their Own Fights?

Is it good for children to settle their problems by tearing each other apart? Absolutely not. When children are allowed to use physical or verbal aggression in their conflicts they learn: it's okay to physically harm another person; it's okay to hurt other people's feelings; it's okay to do anything you want to another person who makes you angry. Destructive behavior of this type directed toward another person leaves children feeling frustrated, because they know they really haven't handled the problem successfully.

Nothing of positive value is learned from vicious fights. Children don't learn "not to fight" the next time or "to love each other more" as a result of a hostile battle. Instead, they are practicing destructive ways to deal with anger. Children should be encouraged to settle their own problems and conflicts, but only if those children possess the necessary skills to do so in a constructive manner.

HOW CAN PARENTS HELP CHILDREN SETTLE CONFLICTS CONSTRUCTIVELY?

Let us imagine two sisters in the middle of a conflict concerning their messy room. They are yelling at each other, throwing toys around the room, and calling each other names. Obviously, the girls do not possess the necessary skills to allow them to settle their conflict in a civil manner. What can the parent do to help the girls deal with their quarreling situation in a constructive manner?

Described below are four methods commonly used by parents in dealing with their children's conflicts. Only one method is likely to help children learn how to solve conflicts arising in the future.

1. Father and Mother decide to let the two girls fight it out on their own. They reason, "Maybe then they will

learn that it isn't much fun to get hurt, and they won't be so quick to fight in the future."

2. Father intercedes, saying, "O.K. girls, if you can't solve this problem within the next three minutes, you will both be grounded for two days."

3. Mother intercedes with no knowledge of what has taken place between the girls prior to the fight, saying, "There you go again, Martha, picking on your sister. It seems that since you are older you could act a little more grown-up!"

4. Father intercedes saying, "It looks like you girls have a problem. You both look pretty mad. Let's see if, together, we can work on this problem. Martha, what are you upset about? How did that make you feel? Why do you think Susan did that? How do you think she felt? Susan, how do you feel about the problem? Would you feel better about the problem if Martha. . . ."

The first solution does not help children learn how to get along better. They are actually encouraged to engage in such fighting techniques simply because their parents condone it by turning their backs on it.

The second solution may be successful in stopping quarreling quickly. However, the girls will remain frustrated and bitter and will release their anger on each other in future bitter quarrels.

The third solution may also end the quarreling quickly but, in the process the older daughter learns that no matter what the reason for the quarrel, she will be blamed. She will feel that her mother is unfair and that she loves her younger sister more. The younger daughter learns that she does not need to be responsible for her quarreling behavior because her older sister always receives the blame. Undoubtedly, these sisters will continue to have intense, bitter quarrels.

The final solution helps children learn acceptable ways

to deal with their anger and solve conflicts constructively. The intervening parent helps his children express their feelings verbally and to understand that they have a right to possess angry feelings, but that they cannot inflict their anger on others.

Such patient efforts *are* time-consuming. However, parents will not need to spend an hour settling *every* quarrel. If they take the time early to help their children learn ways to deal with their angry feelings toward each other, there will be fewer hostile quarrels in the future. Using the model they have learned from their parents, the children will be better able to settle conflicts on their own in constructive ways.

Most parents will readily spend an hour teaching the toddler how to use a spoon. They realize that the time spent teaching now will allow the child to feed himself in the near future. Similarly, time spent teaching children how to "constructively" solve sibling conflicts will allow the children to settle their own sibling conflicts in the future.

chapter 7

Siblings as Targets

In Part One of *Quarreling Kids* we discussed the many reasons why brothers and sisters quarrel. We found that children may engage in sibling conflicts when they:

1. are jealous of their siblings;
2. are pressured by their parents, teachers, and peers;
3. live in a negative home atmosphere;
4. are tired, hungry, ill, or bored;
5. are unable to express their anger in constructive ways.

Notice that the many causes of quarreling listed above share one important element: how children feel about themselves—their self-concepts. When children feel badly about themselves, possessing poor self-concepts, they become frustrated and angry. They express their anger in different ways. The angry, frustrated child may vent his anger on his teachers, peers, or parents; he may kick the cat or break a dish; he may keep anger hidden inside; or, he may, as children often do, express his anger through sibling quarrels.

SIBLINGS: THE IDEAL TARGET

Why do siblings become the target for pent-up frustrations and anger? The child's world consists mainly of teachers, peers, parents, and siblings. When we consider each group as a possible target for anger, we better understand why siblings are often popular targets.

Teachers. The frustrated child considers venting his anger on his teacher if she is the one who caused him to become angry. Depending on the teacher's personality, the angry child might be sent to the principal's office, ridiculed in front of classmates, or rejected by the teacher. Considering these probable consequences, most children decide not to vent anger on teachers.

Peers. The child with angry feelings thinks about venting his anger on his peers. If there is a child in the room who has been designated class scapegoat, he may use that child as someone to attack. The child probably will not vent anger toward those peers with whom he wants to remain friends, since he needs peer acceptance and will not risk losing it by expressing anger.

Parents. Parents do not usually make good targets for a child's pent-up anger. Even when the child's anger is caused by his parents, the child often decides it is too risky to express anger toward them. He thinks they will not approve of such behavior, that they will love him less if he acts hostile toward them, and that they may punish him for such outbursts toward them. Subconsciously the frustrated, angry child thinks: "Parents can hurt you too much. They are not safe targets."

Siblings as Targets. The child with pent-up anger and frustration subconsciously asks, "Who, then, is a safe target?" He often concludes, "Ah-ha! My brothers and sisters are perfect targets. They have low status in the family and do not have enough influence to get me into further trouble."

Thus we find that children often release their angry feelings (caused by many factors) on their siblings, whom they see as relatively safe targets. When all children in the family harbor strong feelings of frustration and anger, there is even greater cause for intense, damaging quarrels.

The illustration on the next page graphically shows how a child's feelings about himself (self-concept) affect his behavior.

The Child's Self-concept, More Than Anything Else, Determines the Amount and Intensity of Quarreling He Does with His Brothers and Sisters.

In Part Two of *Quarreling Kids,* we will study in greater depth the phenomenon known as "self-concept." We will look at a number of ways in which parents can help their children develop self-concepts which are more positive. Children with improved self-concepts have fewer, and less intense, sibling quarrels and are in a better position to develop constructive, warm, loving relationships with their brothers and sisters.

FACTORS AFFECTING SELF-CONCEPT

EXPRESSIONS OF FRUSTRATION
AND ANGER

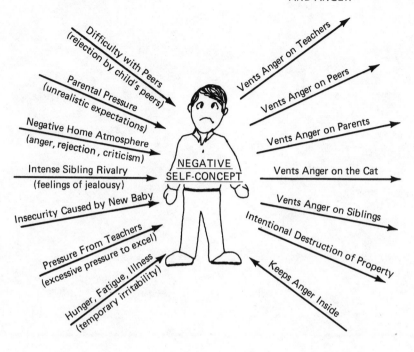

part II

Positive Self-concepts and Quality Sibling Relationships within a Family

chapter 8

The Child's Self-concept

On the previous page is a picture of Carrie, a four-year-old girl with dark brown hair and brown eyes. Carrie's father has a copy of this picture in his wallet which he proudly shares with others. Carrie also has a picture of herself; but it is not a photograph and she does not carry it in her wallet. Carrie's picture of herself has taken four years to develop and is so unique, private, and complex that it could never be captured by a camera.

The photograph at left is an "outside" picture of Carrie. It shows the length of her hair, the color of her skin, and the beauty of her dark brown eyes. The picture which Carrie has is an "inside" picture. What kind of a picture does Carrie have of herself? Does she see herself as independent or dependent, intelligent or stupid, dependable or unreliable, friendly or shy, strong or weak, accepting or rejecting, attractive or unattractive, worthwhile or useless? This "inside" picture reveals more about Carrie and is of greater significance to her life than the "outside" picture which her father carries in his wallet. It influences what she is today and will influence what she becomes tomorrow. This "inside" picture which Carrie has of herself is called her self-concept.

Adults as well as children, have self-concepts. A person's self-concept consists of his own evaluation of all his personal characteristics and qualities. It is his overall "inside" picture: how he sees himself.

The way a person *feels* about his "inside" picture or self-concept is called his *self-esteem*. If the person feels good about himself, we say he has high self-esteem. If he does not feel good about himself, we say he has low self-esteem. The terms *self-concept* and *self-esteem* are similar in meaning and in this book they will be used interchangeably.

WHAT IS THE DIFFERENCE BETWEEN A POSITIVE AND A NEGATIVE SELF-CONCEPT?

Periodically, everyone takes a moment to size themselves up. We all occasionally take a look in the mirror, decide that something needs improvement, and begin a program of diet and exercise. We all occasionally take a look at how we act and decide to try harder to be more understanding, warm, friendly, or more of whatever we find lacking.

Children also size themselves up. They evaluate themselves on a great number of characteristics. Arthur Jersild, the well-known child psychologist and educator, finds that children evaluate themselves on many characteristics, including physical appearance; home and family relationships; enjoyment of recreation; ability in sports, play, and school; intellectual abilities, special talents; personality; character;

emotional tendencies; social relationships and attitudes (Jersild, 1952).

The child's evaluations of his many personal characteristics make up his overall self-concept. To illustrate the way in which children evaluate themselves, look at the following graph, in which twelve-year-old John evaluates himself on some personal qualities:

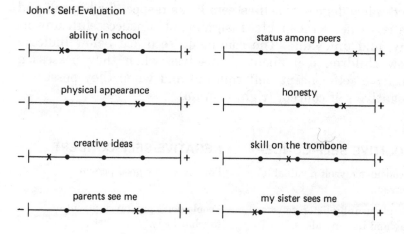

John's Self-Evaluation

John sees himself as a passable student, a rather attractive person, not very creative, a pretty good fellow in the eyes of his parents, well-liked and very popular among his peers, a very honest person, a fair trombone player, and not such a hot brother in his sister's eyes.

Children informally make these kinds of self-evaluations every day. The total of all the child's judgments represents his self-concept. If his overall picture is good, we say the child has a positive self-concept. If the overall picture is poor, we say the child has a negative self-concept. It should be noted, however, that no child has an entirely positive or negative self-concept. Children feel better about themselves in some areas than in others. In John's self-evaluations, he saw himself in a more positive way in some areas (physical appearance, status among peers, honesty, parents' view of him) than in others (ability in school, creative ideas, sister's view of him).

Children who have positive self-concepts see themselves differently than do children with negative self-concepts (Felker, 1974). A child who has a positive self-concept and a high degree of self-esteem respects himself, feels worthy, competent, and lovable. A person who has a negative self-concept and a low degree of self-esteem lacks respect for himself and believes he is incapable, insignificant, unsuccessful, unworthy, and unlovable. The comments recorded below indicate how children feel about themselves when they possess a positive self-concept (left column) and when they possess a negative self-concept (right column).

POSITIVE SELF-CONCEPT	NEGATIVE SELF-CONCEPT
I consider myself a valuable person.	I'm not a very good person.
People usually listen to what I say and like my ideas.	People don't pay much attention to what I say.
I do many things well.	I can't do things very well.
I enjoy new and challenging experiences.	I don't like to do new things because I probably can't do them any way.
I don't get too upset when things don't go exactly right.	I worry a lot about whether I'm doing things right.
I know if I try hard enough I can do almost anything I really want to do.	I doubt if things will ever get any better for me.
Most kids at school like me.	The kids at school pretty much ignore me. I guess they don't like me much.
My parents think I'm a pretty good kid.	My parents don't think I'm worth very much.

It is extremely important that children possess a high degree of self-esteem. Dorothy Briggs, in *Your Child's Self-Esteem,* points out the importance of self-esteem on a child's life with this strong statement:

> *Self-esteem is the mainspring that slates every child for success or failure as a human being* (Briggs, 1975, p. 3).

In order for a child to be a happy, fully functioning individual, he must possess a high degree of self-esteem and a positive self-concept. He must feel competent, worthwhile, and lovable.

HOW DO CHILDREN ACQUIRE THEIR SELF-CONCEPTS?

When the healthy newborn enters the world, he comes equipped with such characteristics as blue, brown, or green eyes, little or no hair, a cute nose, ten fingers, and a voice for crying. He is not, however, born with a ready-made self-concept. Children are not born with wonderfully positive feelings about themselves or feeling they are of little worth and not lovable. Children acquire their self-concepts through encounters with life and people. This process of acquiring a self-concept begins at the moment of birth.

All knowledgeable parents hope their children will acquire positive self-concepts, but find that helping children acquire a positive self-concept requires a lot of effort and wisdom on their part. In order for a child to acquire a positive self-concept, parents must establish and maintain a quality relationship with their child, a relationship which says to the child, "You are wonderful, you are competent, you are worthwhile, you are lovable."

One theory as to how children acquire their self-concept is called the "looking glass" theory. Stated simply, this theory suggests that children learn what kind of person they are by looking into a mirror and seeing a reflected image of themselves. The mirror, in this case, consists of all the significant people in the child's environment. We might call it the child's "environmental mirror."

During the first few years of the child's life, parents are usually the most significant people in the child's environment. Acting as mirrors, parents provide very powerful reflections for their child's development of self-concept. Later the child's mirror includes his teachers, neighbors, relatives, and other children.

Children's feelings about themselves (self-concept) begin to form long before they are old enough to actually understand the words people say to them. The environmental mirror begins working from the moment the baby first meets the world. The infant develops feelings about himself by the way he is touched, held, fed, played with, and bathed. Let us look at the way two mothers provide for their infant's needs. Which mother is fostering a healthy relationship, one which tells the child he is wonderful, competent, worthwhile, and lovable?

> Mother A – *6:00 A.M. – Baby awakens and cries. Mother props a bottle of milk in a holder for Baby and returns to bed. Baby finishes bottle and cries again. Mother changes Baby and places him in a playpen with a few toys while she watches the "Morning Show" on television. Mother prepares Baby's bath and bathes him quickly and silently. Sister arrives home from school and is told to "keep Baby out from under her feet." Mother gives Baby his evening cereal which drools down his chin. Mother impatiently scoops up cereal and repeatedly jams it back in his mouth. This causes Baby to cry. Mother, annoyed by Baby's behavior, jerks him out of the infant seat, puts on his night clothes, puts him in bed and turns out the light.*

> Mother B – *6:00 A.M. – Baby awakens and cries. Mother changes Baby's diaper and holds him closely as she gives him*

the morning feeding. She then rocks him gently over her shoulder, singing in his ear. Baby coos to Mother and she returns the coos. She pats his hands together, bounces him and reacts with smiles and joy. She walks around the house with Baby, offering things for him to touch and bite. During bathtime Mother talks with Baby as she gently washes his body. When Baby splashes the water, Mother laughs at the fun. At lunch Mother patiently scoops cereal off Baby's chin and tries a few times to persuade him to keep the cereal in. Sister arrives home from school. Mother takes a few moments to talk about her day and shows her the things Baby Brother enjoys. Sister plays with Baby, also delighting in his every action. Baby loves all the attention.

Both mothers are influencing their child's development of feelings about himself by the way they provide care for him. The first mother is telling Baby that he is a bother, that he isn't lovable enough to warrant tender words and touching, that he isn't a very good baby because he won't keep his cereal in his mouth, that he is someone who should be dumped in another's care (sister) or dumped in bed as quickly as possible. One cannot help but be saddened by the feelings this baby is developing about himself. This baby's "environmental mirror" is already telling him that he is not very worthwhile or lovable. This baby has already begun to develop a negative self-concept.

Mother B is helping her child develop quite different feelings about himself by the way she cares for him. She is telling him that she enjoys being with him and playing with him because he is lovable, worthwhile enough to warrant her time and attention, brings much joy to family members, and is valued and loved very much. This fortunate baby is already learning good feelings about himself. He is developing a positive self-concept.

In addition to how they touch, hold, play with and care for their child, what parents *say* to their child has a tremendous effect on the feelings he develops about himself. This is true for the two-year-old child, the ten-year-old, and the teen-ager.

Have you ever walked down the aisles in the grocery store and listened to parents conversing with their children? "Stop standing on the front of the cart, you're squashing the bread. Why can't you walk down the aisle like any normal kid?" It is easy to notice the negative comments other people toss at their children and recognize that those comments damage children's self-concepts. It is, however, much more difficult to evaluate what we say to our own children. We think, "Underneath it all my child knows I love him so what I say isn't really all that important." Unfortunately, this is not the case.

What parents say to their children greatly influences the quality of their self-concepts.

WHAT WE SAY TO OUR CHILD AFFECTS HIS SELF-CONCEPT

WHEN WE SAY TO OUR CHILD:	CHILD THINKS:	CHILD FEELS:	AFFECTS SELF-CONCEPT:
"You're six years old now. Why can't you tie your shoes like Susie who is only five?"	I can't tie yet. I'm not good at doing things.	I'm not skillful or competent.	*negatively*
"I think you are old enough to learn how to tie now. Would you like me to show you how?"	I am big enough and smart enough to learn how to tie my shoes.	I can learn new things. I'm competent.	*positively*
"Thank you for setting the table. That helped a lot."	I am helpful.	I'm a worthwhile person.	*positively*

WHEN WE SAY TO OUR CHILD:	CHILD THINKS:	CHILD FEELS:	AFFECTS SELF-CONCEPT:
"I must force you to do anything. I don't know why you have to be so lazy."	I don't have much initiative. I'm lazy.	I'm not a very worthwhile person.	*negatively*
"I saw you out the window trying to make Tommy feel better when he fell down. That was very thoughtful."	I help others. I'm a thoughtful person.	I'm a "good" person.	*positively*
"No one wants to be with you when your face looks like that. Why don't you lay off the junk food?"	I'm ugly. No one wants to be with an ugly.	I'm not very lovable.	*negatively*
"Just you and I are going to spend the day together. What would you like to do?"	Dad wants to be with me all day.	I'm lovable.	*positively*

What we say to our children makes a great deal of difference in how they feel about themselves and whether they feel loved. It is a good idea to check ourselves periodically to find out if we are saying things to our children which help them to feel competent, worthwhile and lovable or to feel just the opposite.

chapter 9

Measures of the Child's Self-concept

It would be helpful to parents to have a simple test which would quickly and accurately give information about the quality of their children's self-concepts. Unfortunately, no such tests are available, because self-concept is very difficult to measure. Measures of self-concept are difficult to obtain because the measuring devices do not always give an accurate picture of how the child views himself. The child can easily bias the results of the measurement either consciously or unconsciously, for instance by saying he has many friends when in fact he feels he has none. Also, a child's self-concept is subject to change, for example, a tired child will test less positively on a self-concept scale.

HOW CAN PARENTS KNOW IF THEIR CHILDREN HAVE POSITIVE OR NEGATIVE SELF-CONCEPTS?

There are three kinds of tools which parents can use to get an idea of how their children feel about themselves. We say an "idea" of how our children feel about themselves, because no test gives absolutely accurate scores of self-concept. We can, however, use the following suggested tools to estimate the status of our children's self-concepts:

1. Direct, informal observations of our children
2. Self-concept evaluation check sheet
3. Family strategies

Direct, Informal Observations of Our Children

Parents can gain information about their children's self-concepts most easily by listening carefully to what their children are saying and how they are acting. To gather information about children's self-concepts, they must know how to listen. Children usually do not openly say, "I'm not important. I feel insecure. I'm not worthwhile." Instead, they express their feelings in subtle ways. Parents must learn how to interpret their children's behaviors and conversations in order to discover how they truly feel about themselves. For example, Susan is nine years old. She is a good student in the fourth grade but lacks confidence in herself. Elizabeth, her sister, is ten and an excellent student in the fifth grade. She is very self-confident and has many academic skills. In school Susan is often reminded by teachers of her older sister's talents: "Nice story, Susan. You know when your sister was in my class she won the writing contest with one of her stories."

One evening as Susan and Elizabeth are drawing pictures together, they argue:

ELIZABETH: I love to draw pictures. Wouldn't it be neat if we could be artists?

SUSAN: Yes, but you have to be really good to be an artist.

ELIZABETH: Mrs. Gillette says my pictures are very good. She said that maybe someday I'll grow up to be a famous artist.

SUSAN: (Laughs at Elizabeth) Oh sure, a famous artist. You can't even draw faces that look like people. Look at that dumb face. (pointing to Elizabeth's picture)

ELIZABETH: You just say that because you can't draw as well as I can.

MOTHER: O.K., that's enough fighting, girls.

Later, Susan scribbles a black X on Elizabeth's drawing and throws it in the trash. Her mother confronts her:

SUSAN: I'm sorry, Mother. I didn't mean to do it.

MOTHER: What do you mean? That X was no accident. Why did you do such a thing? Elizabeth doesn't ruin your drawings does she?

SUSAN: (head drooping) No, I don't know why I did it. (Pause) It just seems like Elizabeth always draws the best pictures.

MOTHER: But your drawings are good, too, Susan.

SUSAN: No they aren't. My pictures are dumb. My stories are dumb. And I'm dumb too.

MOTHER: You are not dumb. You are good at many things.

SUSAN: No I'm not. Just name one thing I do better than Elizabeth. She plays the piano better; she draws better; she gets to play the flute; and she gets a new coat.

This kind of situation between siblings is common in many good homes where parents love their children very much. Susan's parents are puzzled and frustrated by her behavior. They love both girls and try to give them both the same amount of attention. But Susan continues to act as if she is being shortchanged.

The frustrations which Susan's parents feel are very real and quite painful. They love both girls and are trying to provide a happy home for them. Yet, Susan seems very unhappy. Her parents express their frustration, "If only we knew what we are doing wrong with Susan, maybe we could do something to help her."

Surprising as it may seem, Susan is telling her parents why she is so unhappy. She is sending messages through her behavior and through her conversations with others. If we listen to the subtle messages, we hear Susan saying:

I don't think I'm very important. I can't do things as well as other people. I'm not sure of my abilities. Other people don't pay much attention to me. I don't get my fair share, probably because I'm not very worthwhile.

Susan's parents have been unable to decipher her messages and hear what she is saying about herself, because they don't know how to listen to and interpret her camouflaged messages. Thus, they are frustrated because they do not know what the trouble is and cannot help her.

If we listen skillfully, we may find an abundance of information available concerning how our children feel about themselves. Children are always "behaving" and always "communicating." We must take the information they offer, decipher it, and gain some insight into what they are trying to tell us about themselves.

Michael is another child who sends messages about how he feels about himself through his behaviors and communications. One day, Michael is feeling lonely because his mother won't let his friend come to play. Michael limps off to his bedroom and talks to his understanding teddy bear.

> *Teddy, will you be my friend? I'm a good friend. I play good. I don't hit you. I don't kick you. I don't bite you. And I have lots of brains, too, so I can teach you everything about dinosaurs. I'm strong—I won't even let the dinosaurs eat you. You would like me to be your friend, Teddy. And Mrs. Johnston says I'm a good helper at pick-up time.*

In this short plea for friendship, Michael tells us that he views himself as someone who:

–plays nicely with others. "I play good. I don't hit you. I don't bite you."

–is quite intelligent. "I have lots of brains, too, so I can teach you everything about dinosaurs."

–is strong and protective. "I'm so strong I won't even let the dinosaurs eat you."

–is dependable and helpful. "Mrs. Johnston says I'm a good helper at pick-up time."

–is worthwhile enough to make a good friend. "You would like me to be your friend, Teddy."

A sensitive listener interprets Michael's messages to mean Michael feels pretty good about himself. He appears to have a positive self-concept. The way an individual sees himself may be very similar to the way other people see him. If Michael really does play nicely with others and is intelligent, strong, dependable and helpful, then other children and adults probably look at him positively, also.

However, some children possess views of themselves (self-concept) which are quite different from the way others see them (revealed self). Such is the case of sixteen-year-old Marie. Teachers describe Marie as a very pretty girl who is a little shy. Although Marie does not participate in any school social activities, she is well liked by her peers. Marie works hard in school and is a 'B' student.

Marie's view of herself is quite different from that of her teachers'. Marie complains to her mother:

> *None of the kids like me, probably because I'm so short and so dumb. Other kids have time to be in clubs and goof off with their friends, but I always have to study. I wish I weren't so dumb. Maybe if I were smarter, kids would like me more.*

There is a wide discrepancy between the way Marie sees herself and the way others see her. Marie sees herself as unattractive, not intelligent, and disliked by her peers. Others see Marie as attractive and a hard-working, good student who is liked by her peers. If this discrepancy between Marie's real self-concept and her revealed self-concept goes unnoticed, people around Marie will not actively try to help Marie develop a more positive self-concept because they do not realize that she needs help. They think she already has positive feelings about herself.

Let us look at the behaviors of three children, two with very positive self-concepts and a high degree of self-esteem. We begin with Katie, a child who is busily engaged in the activities of her kindergarten class:

TEACHER: You have colored paper for your feathers and brown paper for the headband. Does anyone have an idea how to make feathers look real?

KATIE: (volunteers) You can cut tiny little cuts all around the feathers. It makes it look like real hairs on the feather.

TEACHER: Yes, that is called fringe. It is a little hard to cut fringe, so if anyone needs help just raise your hand.

KATIE: (painstakingly cuts fringe around the feathers and talks to a friend) You make good fringe, Angela. I make good fringe too. It's hard, but we can do it, can't we?

TEACHER: When you are ready to attach the feathers, you may use my stapler, tape, or glue.

KATIE: I'm going to 'stample' mine. I never did that before. (Katie tries to staple the feathers but each time the feather slips and is attached crooked. She takes the feathers off and tries again several times.) This sure is hard but if I practice it, the feathers will stay on.

KATIE: Look, Teacher, I 'stampled' my feathers. (beaming with pride) Now I'm going to show Angela how to 'stample' hers.

This brief glimpse of Katie as she participates in her daily school life shows that she:

−has self-confidence. "This sure is hard but if I practice, the feathers will stay on."

−seeks to be independent. "It's hard but we can do it, can't we?"

−handles failure well. (Crooked feathers do not defeat her.)

−is responsible and completes tasks. (The feathers finally stay on. She painstakingly cuts fringe around all the feathers.)

−provides self with positive feedback on skills. "I make good fringe, too."

−takes pride in accomplishments. "Look, Teacher, I 'stampled' my feathers."

−relates well to others. "You make good fringe, Angela."

−tries new experiences. "I'm going to 'stample' mine. I never did that before."

−expresses own ideas. "You can cut tiny little cuts all around the feathers. It makes it look like real hairs on the feathers."

−is persistent. "This sure is hard but if I practice, the feathers will stay on."

There can be little doubt that Katie views herself as being a worthwhile person with many skills. Katie's behavior indicates that she possesses a high degree of self-esteem.

Let us look at the behaviors of ten-year-old Phillip. Phillip is the youngest in a family of seven children. When he was four years old, all of his brothers and sisters were in school and he played alone most of the day. Phillip's mother felt that he needed to be with other children his own age, so she enrolled him in nursery school. He clung to her and cried when she left him at school everyday for the first two weeks.

For several days Phillip would not take his coat off and stood by the lockers most of the morning. He watched the other children playing and hung his head when anyone approached. After several weeks, Phillip did sit with the other children during group time, but would not sing, dance, or share experiences with the group.

By the end of the year, Phillip would not paint at the easel if anyone appeared to be watching him. He once tried to cut paper flowers but found it difficult and would not continue, even when help was offered. Phillip would not play with other children, although he did talk with one girl who seemed to sense his fear and try to comfort him.

Phillip's fourth grade teacher reports that he is now a good student and finishes all of his work neatly. On the few occasions that he misses an answer, he becomes nervous and self-conscious. He does not enjoy gym time. It is difficult to tell if Phillip is liked by the other children in his class, because he is generally left to himself. Phillip's teacher says, "I don't really know how Phillip feels about himself because he so rarely says anything to anyone."

Although Phillip "rarely says anything," he is still revealing much about how he feels about himself. Phillip's actions indicate that he has very little confidence in himself. He refuses to participate in new experiences, because the possibility of failure is too painful. He offers no ideas of his own, because he feels his ideas are not worth offering. He quits on difficult tasks, because he lacks confidence in his abilities and will not risk failure. He shies away from other children, because he is afraid that others may not accept him.

It is obvious that Phillip has low self-esteem. Although he is a good student, is dependable and produces neat work, his total picture of himself is not positive. He unconsciously focuses on his inabilities and behaves in terms of his judgments of self in those areas. Phillip does not view his well-developed skills (academic achievement, dependability, and neatness) as being sufficient to warrant a self-evaluation of "worthwhile individual." Thus, he is shy, insecure, and afraid, behaving as though he were of little worth.

In contrast, some children possess limited skills but still see themselves as worthwhile persons. These children are able to focus on the positive aspects of their judgments of self and act in reference to them. They may rate themselves as poor in many areas, but still possess a high degree of self-esteem. Such is the case of sixteen-year-old Mark, a junior in high school. National achievement test scores place Mark in the lower third of his class in reading comprehension and math skills. Due to a farm accident when he was thirteen, Mark lost the sight in one eye.

Mark is an ambitious young man. This past year he served as chief photographer for the school newspaper. He was very dependable and always met newspaper deadlines with photographs complete and well-done.

Mark is very confident and shows leadership qualities. His peers elected him vice-president of the junior class.

Since his accident, Mark has not been able to continue in football and basketball, and has chosen another sport in which he can excel: running. He runs five miles a day and is a valuable member of the cross-country team. Mark appears to be realistic about his intellectual abilities. He knows he is not good in math, but is proud that he can drive and fix a tractor. Mark plans to go into farming with his father after graduation.

On the basis of his physical and intellectual characteristics, we might expect that Mark would possess a low degree of self-esteem and a poor self-concept. We might even predict that he would have a difficult time with life due to his physical disability and low academic aptitude.

Instead, Mark's case illustrates that individuals with mental or physical disabilities need not necessarily have low self-esteem. A child does not have to be excellent in all areas in order to have a positive self-concept. The child who is less than perfect is not doomed to a negative view of himself.

Self-concept Evaluation
Checklist

Although you have never seen or talked with the children described in the previous pages, you can gain a general idea of the quality of their self-concepts by looking at their behavior—what they say and how they act. Similarly, it is possible to learn about your own children's self-concepts by observing their behavior. The difficulty comes in trying to observe them objectively. If we see *only* our children's negative behavior we may conclude that they have poor self-concepts, conversely, if we ignore signs of their having a negative self-concept we may, falsely, conclude that they have positive feelings about themselves.

When asked, "Does your child have a positive self-concept?" many parents reply, "Well, I'm not sure. I think my child does, but sometimes he does things or says things which make me wonder. How can I tell how my child feels about himself?"

It is not possible to obtain a comprehensive, completely valid measure of our children's self-concepts. However, it is possible, through observations, to gain a general idea of the status of our children's self-concepts.

The checklist which follows contains a number of traits which are related to self-concept. Place an X next to those items which are characteristic of your child. Leave blank those items which are not characteristic of your child.*

For some items you may find that your child is usually like this but that there are a few occasions when he or she is not. Mark all items as though you were saying "Generally speaking, my child is_____."

The self-concept evaluation checklist can be used to obtain a *general idea* of the condition of your child's self-concept. Those items listed in the left column are characteristics commonly found in children with positive self-concepts. Those items listed in the right column are characteristics commonly found in children with negative self-concepts.

If your child possesses many of the traits from the left column, there is reason to believe that he has positive feelings about himself. He feels competent, worthwhile, and lovable.

If your child possesses many of the traits from the right column there is reason to believe that he may possess negative feelings about himself. He may feel that he is not competent, not very worthwhile, and not an O.K. person.

---

*The items on this checklist are most appropriate for children over the age of six. Before the age of six the child cannot be expected to have integrated the social skills listed. The very young child's self-concept is still very much in the process of being formed. Self-centered and dependent behaviors are a normal and necessary part of this stage of development and should not be viewed as an indication of a negative self-concept.

*SELF-CONCEPT EVALUATION CHECKLIST

Generally speaking, my child possesses these traits:

_____ acts friendly toward others	_____ brags excessively
_____ seems self-confident	_____ seems overly critical of others
_____ gets along well with siblings	_____ appears very shy
_____ shows enthusiasm for life	_____ makes "fun" of others
_____ engages in constructive activities	_____ seems afraid to try new things
_____ appears caring of others	_____ feels that he usually gets shortchanged
_____ readily offers a helping hand to others	_____ engages in excessive daydreaming
_____ shows a loving attitude toward others	_____ seems overly reluctant to meet new people
_____ has a positive attitude about most things	_____ keeps anger bottled up inside
_____ seems relatively outgoing	_____ exhibits angry defiance of parents and teachers
_____ laughs easily with others	_____ often seems depressed
_____ looks forward to a new day	_____ attacks others verbally and/ or physically
_____ is sensitive toward other's feelings	_____ gives up easily
_____ gets along well with peers	_____ keeps to himself most of the time
_____ doesn't get overly upset when things don't turn out well	_____ needles and antagonizes others
_____ approaches new experiences with confidence	_____ initiates most quarrels with his siblings
_____ seems supportive of others	_____ engages in destructive activities
_____ engages actively with people and projects	_____ has a negative attitude toward most things
_____ appears happy	_____ unable to accept failure
_____ shows stick-to-itiveness in most endeavors	_____ takes on the role of "class clown"
_____ expresses anger in constructive ways	_____ acts passive and lethargic
_____ gets along well with teachers	_____ seems overly jealous of siblings
_____ expresses feelings openly	_____ appears to feel inferior

*Compiled by Leah Acus, for use in *Quarreling Kids,* 1981.

Family Strategies

Parents can gain information about their children's self-concepts by participating in informal, gamelike activities with family members. In addition, children can learn and benefit from discovering that their parents, also, possess negative feelings about themselves as well as positive ones.

ABOUT ME

About Me (Part One)—Each member of the family evaluates himself on the characteristics listed below. This can be done by asking each person to comment on the first item (friendly). Then, each person in turn comments on the second item (truthful), etc., throughout the list of characteristics.

Self-evaluations are done on a scale of 1-5. A "one" rating indicates the person believes he possesses very little of this characteristic. A "five" rating indicates the person believes this item is *very* characteristic of him.

Some children may not want to evaluate themselves openly on the listed characteristics in front of all family members. They may feel more comfortable sharing their evaluations with just one understanding and sensitive parent.

A parent may need to explain the meaning of some items to younger children (i.e., "confident means you think you are able to do many things").

Generally speaking, on a scale of 1-5, I consider myself to be a person who is:

1) _____ Friendly
   1   2   3   4   5
2) _____ Truthful
   1   2   3   4   5
3) _____ Happy
   1   2   3   4   5
4) _____ Good working with my hands
   1   2   3   4   5
5) _____ Confident
   1   2   3   4   5
6) _____ Physically attractive
   1   2   3   4   5

7)						Organized
	1	2	3	4	5	
8)						Even-tempered
	1	2	3	4	5	
9)						Optimistic about the future
	1	2	3	4	5	
10)						Intelligent
	1	2	3	4	5	
11)						Kind
	1	2	3	4	5	
12)						Productive
	1	2	3	4	5	
13)						Well-liked by others
	1	2	3	4	5	
14)						A good student
	1	2	3	4	5	
15)						Enthusiastic about life now
	1	2	3	4	5	
16)						Sensitive to other's feelings
	1	2	3	4	5	
17)						Athletically inclined
	1	2	3	4	5	
18)						Creative
	1	2	3	4	5	
19)						Musically inclined
	1	2	3	4	5	
20)						Thought well of by his father
	1	2	3	4	5	
21)						Thought well of by his mother
	1	2	3	4	5	
22)						Thought well of by his brothers and/or sisters
	1	2	3	4	5	
23)						Thought well of by his teachers
	1	2	3	4	5	

Interpretation. If most of your child's self-evaluations lie in the upper half of the rating scale (3–5), he is very likely a person who possesses positive feelings about himself. He has a positive self-concept.

About Me (Part Two)—List five words or phrases which best describe you. You may choose items from the list above or think of other words which better describe you.

1) _____
2) _____
3) _____
4) _____
5) _____

About Me (Part Three)—Select five characteristics from the list of twenty-three above about which you would like to feel better. Why do you think these characteristics are important?

1) _____
2) _____
3) _____
4) _____
5) _____

1)_____   2)_____   3)_____   4)_____   5)_____

About Me (Part Four)—Rate yourself on a scale of 1-10 on the three items listed below:

I am a competent person.

1	2	3	4	5	6	7	8	9	10

I am a worthwhile person.

1	2	3	4	5	6	7	8	9	10

I am a likeable person.

1	2	3	4	5	6	7	8	9	10

chapter 10

Effects of Children's Self-concepts on Sibling Relationships

We have considered a number of factors which contribute to the quarreling of brothers and sisters: sibling rivalry; pressure from parents, teachers, and peers; temporary irritability; home atmosphere; inability to handle anger constructively; and especially the *condition of children's self-concepts*. Nathaniel Branden has called self-concept the single most significant key to a person's behavior (Branden, 1969). **The child's self-concept, more than anything else, determines the amount and intensity of quarreling he or she does with his or her brothers and sisters.**

HOW DOES THE SELF-CONCEPT AFFECT SIBLING RELATIONSHIPS?

Most children are found somewhere between the two extremes of positive and negative self-concepts. The way a child feels about himself changes slightly from day to day. Larger changes in the child's self-concept, both positive and negative, may occur over a period of years. Changes in children's self-concepts result in improvement or deterioration of sibling relationships over periods of time.

Condition of Self-concept	Possible Behaviors	Sibling Relationship
Positive self-concept Feels good about himself—worthwhile and lovable	Positive outlook on life—friendly, caring, supportive	Warm, loving, supportive, caring, constructive behaviors (mostly quarrels of the nuisance variety)
Negative Self-concept Views self as stupid, unlovable, worthless	Negative outlook on life—antagonizes others, offers putdowns	Long-term, hostile, destructive quarreling

CHILDREN WHO FEEL GOOD ABOUT THEMSELVES

When children feel good about themselves, they have a solid base upon which other positive learning experiences can be built. They are secure, self-confident, happy, and expect good things to happen to them. Because of their positive approach to life and people, they generally experience happy, healthy relationships with others.

Such children have much less difficulty getting along with their brothers and sisters. Because they have a positive view of themselves, they are able to have a positive view of their brothers and sisters. They enjoy their siblings' company, offer support to their shared activities, and show genuine concern and encouragement toward them. When all children in a family have positive views of themselves, the family is very likely to experience strong, happy, loving relationships.

Positive Self-concept and Supportive Sibling Relationships

Children who have a positive self-concept find it uncomfortable to attack, criticize, and initiate quarrelsome relationships with their siblings. These children have no need for intense, long-term, damaging fights. The minor squabbles which do occur, and can be cured without too much difficulty, are usually brought on by physical causes: lack of sleep, hunger, or chronic illness discussed in Chapter Five.

The scene which follows illustrates the warm, loving relationships which can exist among siblings who possess a positive view of themselves. It is a true episode in the lives of three children.

KAREN: (nine-year-old) Mom, can we use your markers to draw planets? I'm going to teach Sara about space.

MOTHER: I think Sara would like that. The markers are on my desk. Be sure to put the caps back on.

KAREN: We will. (Rushes downstairs to the playroom carrying three encyclopedias, paper, and markers)

SARA: (four-year-old) I want to carry something too.

KAREN: Here, you carry the paper and markers. You're big enough, aren't you?

SARA: Yes, and I'm big enough to learn about planets too, aren't I?

KAREN: You sure are. You have to be smart to learn about planets. There are nine planets. I'm going to teach you all of them. There's even one called Pluto (laughs), but it's not a dog.

SARA: Pluto, that's a funny name. (Both girls laugh. They spend an hour together. Karen shows Sara pictures in the encyclopedia, telling her about the different planets. Sara listens attentively. Karen, playing the part of the teacher, draws circles to represent the planets. She instructs Sara to cut each planet out as she tapes them in order on the wall.)

KAREN: Boy, you sure are good at cutting, Sara.

SARA: Yes, but it's hard to cut the little ones.

KAREN: Do you want me to cut the little ones for you?

SARA: No, I can do it by myself.

KAREN: Yes, you are big enough. (Paper planets completed, Karen decides to quiz Sara over what she has taught her.) Now I'm going to ask you some questions about planets. What is the biggest planet?

SARA: Jupiter.

KAREN: Right, now what planet is furthest from the sun?

SARA: Mars.

KAREN: No, it's Pluto, remember the dog? O.K., what planet do we live on?

SARA: (smiles) Michigan.

KAREN: No, we live in Michigan but our planet is called Earth. (Karen looks at Sara's sad face and tries to comfort her.) Hey, that was pretty good. You knew that we live in Michigan. Let's go show Greg the planets you made. He won't believe it.

SARA: (Gathers up the planets and runs to find Greg. She finds him playing the piano and excitedly interrupts his piece.) Look Greg, I made all the planets. You want me to count them for you?

GREG: (fourteen years old) You made all the planets? Wow, that must have been hard work.

SARA: It took a long time. (Spreads the planets out on the floor and counts all nine), And this is the biggest one.

GREG: Sara, that is really neat. You sure do make good planets, don't you?

SARA: (smiling with pride) I sure do. Do you want me to make some planets for you?

GREG: Yes, would you? I would really like that.

SARA: I will, but first I have to make some for Mommy and Daddy and my friend Kristi. I'm going to teach Kristi all about planets too. She is younger than I am, you know.

Throughout this brief episode, there is much evidence of encouragement and enthusiasm over another's success; sensitivity and caring toward the feelings of others; and genuine warmth and love among the siblings. There are moments during the conversations of these children which were invitations to ridicule. The expected verbal attack did not occur, however. We find, instead, evidence of warm relationships existing among the three children.

Genuine caring, giving, praise, joy, encouragement, sensitivity, and love come from children who possess positive self-concepts. Their need of self-esteem has been satisfied. They are happy with themselves and behave in normal, socially acceptable ways.

CHILDREN WHO DO NOT FEEL GOOD ABOUT THEMSELVES

What happens to children whose need for self-esteem is not satisfied, children with poor self-concepts? They have feelings of inferiority, weakness, and helplessness. As a result of these feelings, a number of things may happen to them. They may become emotionally withdrawn, passive, aggressive, anxious, compulsive, or depressed.

SELF-CONCEPT	BEHAVIOR
"I don't get along well with other kids. They don't like me very much."	→ Needles and antagonizes until quarrels and fights are initiated.
"I can't do things very well. I have no talent. I'm really just a dummy."	→ Degrades and makes fun of other's work (unconsciously thinking his work will fare better in comparison).
"I'm not a very responsible person."	→ Does not complete tasks.
"People are always taking advantage of me."	→ Is unfair in his dealings with others.
"I'm just plain stupid."	→ Does not attempt class assignments. Does poorly in school.
"I'm not a very attractive person."	→ Dresses poorly.

Children who are emotionally withdrawn, due to low self-esteem, often have strong fears of personal inadequacy. They find relationships with people so painful that they withdraw from them, and fear criticism and rejection.

Low self-esteem causes some children to become passive and unable to express their assertive and aggressive feelings, thus keeping their anger bottled up. Passive children are "allergic" to anger and do whatever they can to avoid it. They are on an endless treadmill of pleasing other people, so that other people will treat them well and they will avoid anger.

Anxious Children have marked feelings of inadequacy and lack confidence in themselves. They feel that they have little ability and fear being tested against the performance of others. They do not feel valued, wanted, and worthwhile.

Compulsive Children often feel unworthy and exert great energy into projects in order to prove their worthiness to others.

Depressed Children have a depreciated view of themselves. They feel inadequate and inferior to others.

Overly-aggressive Children react to interpersonal problems with angry outbursts and undue aggressiveness. They explode in frequent temper tantrums, and angrily defy their parents and siblings.

All of the behaviors briefly described above are closely related to low self-esteem or poor self-concept. The behavior which we will consider in greater depth is excessive aggressive behavior, for it points directly to the thesis that poor self-concept and low self-esteem yield intense fighting and quarreling among siblings.

LOW SELF-ESTEEM AS FERTILE
GROUND FOR SIBLING QUARRELS

In the next brief episode we learn much about the self-concepts of two brothers, Shawn, age 9 and Billy, age 11. They are aggressive toward each other, berate each other's character, and experience much difficulty in their relations with each other. Dialogues such as the one below occur several times daily in their home:

SHAWN: Mom, why do I have to take the trash out? I did it last week. It's not fair.

BILLY: Oh, no you didn't. You took some of it out, but I had to take the rest.

SHAWN: Big deal, you only took one bag out.

BILLY: So it's your turn again.

SHAWN: Just because you take one bag out, you think it's my turn. You're so dumb. Don't ever ask me to help you do anything, 'cause I won't.

(The brothers are sent to wash their hands before dinner. There is much pushing and hitting in the bathroom.)

MOTHER: What is going on in there?

BILLY: Shawn hit me.

SHAWN: Yeah, because you splashed water all over my shirt.

BILLY: It was an accident. My hand slipped.

SHAWN: Oh sure it was. Was it an accident when you hit Ben today and had to stay after school? You're always causing trouble and getting into fights. Nobody can stand you.

(Father orders the boys to the table and demands that there be no more fighting.)

MOTHER: Why do you boys fight so much? Your cousins Mark and Michael don't fight.

BILLY: Maybe it's because Mark isn't dumb like Shawn.

SHAWN: I'm not dumb. You're the one who is going to flunk sixth grade.

FATHER: I can't take any more of this. All you do is fight. Both of you go to your rooms. Then maybe we can have some peace and quiet.

Why is there so much quarreling and fighting between these brothers? There are undoubtedly a number of causes, but the one which most dramatically affects their relationship is that both boys possess negative self-concepts. **Children who do not feel good about themselves cannot feel good about others**. Erik Fromm, the well-known psychologist, says that we cannot love others unless we have a healthy love of ourselves (Jersild, 1952). Shawn and Billy feel so much inner pain, caused by their bad feelings about themselves, that they cannot focus on developing warm, loving relationships with each other.

In homes where the children have negative self-concepts, there will be more fighting and quarreling among siblings. Children who feel that they are not likeable and not worthwhile often become aggressive and hostile, have more angry outbursts, and quarrel more with their brothers and sisters.

CHANGES IN SELF-CONCEPTS AND SIBLING QUARRELING

The "Go-Round"

Think back a few years to the playground and remember the "go-round" which was set in motion by your running feet and then continued to circle as you hopped aboard. Once set in motion, the circling go-round was difficult, although not impossible, to stop.

Two such self-perpetuating "go-rounds" are illustrated below. Parents may, unintentionally, direct their child to the "negative" go-round, or they may extend the much-needed

NEGATIVE GO-ROUND

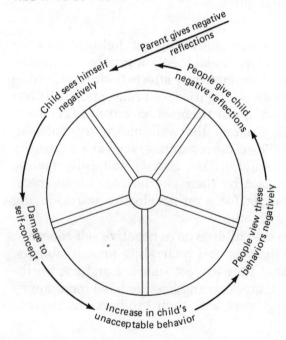

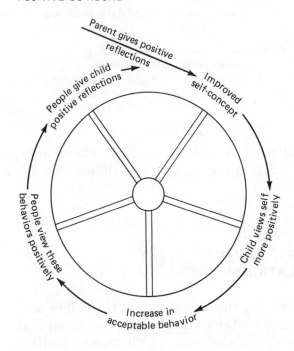

energy necessary to make sure their child gets aboard the "positive" go-round.

Children aboard the negative, self-perpetuating go-round feel so badly about themselves that they resort to intense, long-term fighting with their siblings. Children aboard the positive, self-perpetuating go-round feel good about themselves, and are able to develop constructive, warm, loving relationships with their brothers and sisters.

Relationships among siblings in one family change from day to day and from year to year. When the environment enhances the self-concepts of children in a family, there will be a resulting improvement in the relationships among those children. If the environment changes so that the children's

As children's self-concepts become more positive	→	Improved sibling relationships, less quarreling and fighting among siblings
As children's self-concepts become more negative	→	Deterioration of sibling relationships, increase in quarreling and fighting among siblings.

self-concepts are affected negatively, there is likely to be more quarreling and fighting among the siblings in the family.

RELATIONSHIP BETWEEN CHILDREN'S SELF-CONCEPTS AND SIBLING RELATIONSHIPS

When we understand the importance of the child's self-concept in determining his behavior it becomes apparent that the improvement of a child's self-concept will make a positive difference in the quality of his relationships with his siblings. **The most effective way to improve sibling relationships is to improve each child's self-concept**.

In the remaining chapters, we will discuss specific ways in which parents can help their children develop positive self-concepts and foster loving sibling relationships within the family.

chapter 11

Helping Your Child Recognize His Skills

Children develop skills in many areas. Unfortunately, some children continually feel that others are more skillful, and thus more worthwhile, than themselves. Such was the case with John:

John, a precocious boy, learned Latin, French, Dutch, and Spanish before entering college. He enrolled in Harvard and graduated after only two years, a member of Phi Beta Kappa. His accomplishments were numerous. He held more important government offices than anyone else in the history of the United States. And yet, shortly before his death, he wrote, " . . . my whole life has been a succession of disappointments. I can scarcely recollect a single instance of success in anything that I ever undertook." The man was John Quincy Adams, sixth president of the United States (Kennedy, 1956).

How can it be that such an accomplished man as John Quincy Adams felt he had done nothing very worthwhile? Why do some children who possess many skills still feel that are not very worthwhile?

Children sometimes feel inadequate because they think they have no talents or skills. Or, if they do recognize their skills, they do not consider them important enough to feel good about. This inaccurate self-evaluation sometimes occurs because at some time in the child's life his "environmental mirror," or the significant people in his life, have sent messages to him which say, "You are not a skillful person." Emotionally stable parents, of course, do not deliberately try to make their child feel incompetent and lacking in skills. Unfortunately, however, even well-meaning parents sometimes unintentionally transmit such messages to their children.

EMPHASIS ON ACADEMICS

Sometimes parents put such heavy emphasis on academic skills they fail to recognize other areas in which a child may be skillful, or think of the other areas as less important and not worthy of much attention. These parents deliver the messages that the child's chosen skills are of little value and don't contribute to their considering him worthwhile. His environmental mirror says that only academic talent has worth. If the child doesn't feel skillful in academic areas, he labels himself as incompetent and not worthwhile.

For example, Steve is a fine boy who happens to be skillful in a non-academic skill area. Steve could be found most weekends busily working in the garage. He loved to design and build model cars, bookends, and small furniture. He was very creative and had real talent in woodworking. He often worked nonstop to finish a project which would make him late for dinner and greatly disturb his mother. His father complained endlessly of the messy workbench and often reminded Steve, "If you would spend as much time on schoolwork as you do playing around with tools, you would be more successful in school." Steve's parents were sending the message, "You aren't skillful or worthwhile because you don't do well in school."

After many such damaging messages had been sent, Steve stopped working in the area in which he was skillful. Then, his mother did not have to nag him to come to dinner on time because he was draped over a nearby chair staring out the window. His father did not have to complain about misplaced tools because Steve no longer used tools. Giving up woodworking should have allowed more time for study and improved grades. Instead, Steve's grades grew worse.

Certainly, Steve's parents wanted the best for their son, but because they saw academic skills as the only measure of competence, they made Steve feel he was not a skillful or worthwhile person. Because Steve did not feel worthwhile, he lacked the confidence to try anything—woodworking or academic pursuits.

In contrast, a second grader named David did not know the names of the colors (unknown to the teacher was the fact that he was colorblind), was not in the highest reading group, and always came in last in races across the playground. Still, David managed to have very good feelings about himself. He believed he possessed many important skills and felt like a worthwhile person. David was good at driving a tractor; he was persistent in building a chicken coop one summer; and he played the piano well for his age.

His parents were wise enough to recognize his skills in non-academic areas. They also, of course, thought academic skills were important and hoped he would do well in school. They saw their son as a skillful person and passed that image on to him. The boy who did not appear to possess much skill in academic areas as a nine-year-old continued to feel confident and good about himself. Today, he is a skillful physician and my husband. David continues to believe he is a worthwhile person just as his parents did many years ago.

HELPING YOUR CHILD DISCOVER
SKILLS

Skill areas include anything constructive which gives the child a feeling of success and competence: singing, sketching, mechanics, babysitting, woodworking, getting along with people, mothering, carrying out responsibilities, swimming, helping elderly people, gaining knowledge through reading, driving a car, collecting rocks, and so on. Anything constructive which a child likes to do, feels is important, and receives satisfaction from, is a skill area in which he can learn to feel competent, skillful, and worthwhile. It is important for parents to help their child recognize the many skills he possesses so that he can feel competent and worthwhile. When the child realizes that he is skillful in many areas, he learns to feel competent and worthwhile.

Every child needs to have others recognize his skills and competencies. This is illustrated vividly by the child who says to his mother: "Let's play darts, Mother. I'll throw the darts, and you say 'Wonderful!' " When this mother exclaims "Wonderful!" at her child's dart throwing, she helps him identify something he does well. She helps him feel competent and good about himself. A child does many things every day which provide opportunities for parents to help him see himself as skillful and worthwhile:

When the parent says:	*The child thinks:*
"You sure learned how to use that stapler fast" to the five-year-old."	"I'm good at using a stapler. I learn things fast. I'm competent."
"You handled those icy roads well, Paul."	"I'm a skillful driver."
"I bet the rabbits like the job you did on their cage."	"I did a good job of cleaning. I'm a good worker."

Simple messages like these help children identify their skills and contribute to their total feeling of being worthwhile.

A Blank Environmental Mirror

Children continually check their "environmental mirror" to find out what kind of person they are. In some homes parents are, unfortunately, too busy to notice their child's strengths or do not realize the importance of providing positive feedback to their child concerning his competencies. In such situations, the child is denied a source of helpful information about himself. He checks his environmental mirror and finds no image. Even though the child may be very skillful and competent, he is denied the opportunity to see himself as such.

Pushing for Excellence in Skill Areas

Parents who push their children to be the "best" compared to others often condemn them to feelings of low self-esteem.

For example, Karen is an attractive girl with an A—average. She is a member of the choir and participates in cross-country track.

Despite the many activities in which she excels, Karen does not feel skillful or competent. Her parents provide voice lessons, weeks at summer sports camps, and an expensive study area for Karen. Karen's low self-esteem probably stems from the fact that her parents do more than "encourage" her, they push her. No matter how well she does in school, her parents expect her to do better. Although it is not explicitly said, Karen is well aware that her parents want her to be valedictorian next year. She knows they will think more of her if she is chosen to sing the solo at the Spring Concert.

Karen's parents are sending indirect, damaging messages which say, "We expect you to be the best at everything you do. We give you wonderful opportunities (lessons, camps, material comforts), but you never quite measure up." Karen knows she is not the best at anything and feels she is letting her parents down. She feels she is not very worthwhile because she does not meet her parents' unrealistic expectations.

WHOOO, WHOOO, WHO ARE YOU?

The object of the Owl game is to help family members think about their own skills and interests as well as the skills and interests of other family members. Children will be surprised at the number of skills they actually possess. They may discover that their parents also think they are quite competent and worthwhile. Parents can learn the interests and skill areas of their children which they can later support and encourage.

Directions: Family members sit in a circle. One person volunteers to be the Owl. The Owl chooses another member of the family and says to him "Who, who, who are you?" That person replies, "I am a person who _____," completing the sentence by telling one of his interests or skills.

All replies must be positive. Negative evaluations of one's self such as "I'm a person who gets bad grades" are not acceptable. Instead, the person might reply "I'm a person who likes to play tennis," or "I'm a person who is good at making peanut butter cookies." The Owl asks the same person again, "Who, who, who are you?" This time the person might say "I'm a person who likes to go fishing." The Owl continues asking "who" questions to the same person until that person has identified fifteen interests or skills he possesses. (A smaller number may be used for young children.) Then, the person who has just answered fifteen questions becomes the Owl and asks fifteen "who" questions of another family member. The game continues until every family member has been both the Owl and the answering person.

Interpretation. If some members of the family have difficulty answering fifteen "who" questions, others should help by offering ideas about that person's skills. When the family quickly and honestly identifies more skills which they think the person possesses, they help the person to recognize and accept them as being part of his total self. As a result of this simple game, the person's self-concept becomes a little more positive.

ACCENTUATING THE POSITIVE

Admittedly, it is not easy being a parent. Making sure our children grow to be healthy, productive adults, able to cope with life, is an awesome responsibility. The realization of this tremendous responsibility sometimes turns spontaneous, warm parents into computerlike robots who evaluate their children's every move and provide continual printouts detailing their every weakness. Shortcomings are immediately pointed out to the child.

When a child's environmental mirror reflects only his shortcomings and does not acknowledge any of his skills and competencies, the child begins to see himself as a person with few skills who is not very worthwhile. These feelings can occur in a child who in reality possesses many strengths and competencies, simply because the people around him do not reflect a positive image back to him. The fact that many people are raised under such circumstances is reflected in the findings of *The Human Potentialities Research Project*, which states that, "The average, healthy, well-functioning person has a very limited awareness of his personality strengths and resources but has a much clearer idea of his weaknesses and problem areas" (Otto, Mahn, 1968, p. 143).

Is your child more aware of his weaknesses than of his strengths? To gain an idea, try this quick exercise. Draw a line down the middle of a piece of paper (top to bottom). Label the left column "STRENGTHS-ASSETS." Label the right column "SHORTCOMINGS-WEAKNESSES." Tomorrow morning begin the day by writing down all the comments you make to your child which gives him information about either his strengths or weaknesses. Don't contaminate the data by carefully guarding your words. Try to say what you would normally say during a typical day with your child.

At the end of the day, take your list into a quiet room and tally the results. Most papers will fall off the right side of the table. This does not mean you are a bad parent, but perhaps that you are a very conscientious parent trying hard to offer direction to your child so he can grow to be a healthy functioning adult.

One mother included these comments on her list during the hour before her daughter left for school. Looking over her list made her realize how many negative comments she gave her daughter, when she meant only to be helpful.

This experiment is meant to emphasize an important point: under the weight of the heavy responsibilities of parenting, we sometimes focus too intently on our children's shortcomings and unintentionally deliver messages to them which say, "You have a lot of faults and aren't too skillful." We must endeavor to shift our comments to the positive side of the paper, by giving feedback to children which says, "You are a worthwhile person."

Most children are already very much aware of their shortcomings. They are, however, not always aware of their strengths. Children who know only their weaknesses feel weak, while children who are aware of their assets are in a better position to identify and work on the shortcomings. Our job as parents is to help them recognize their strengths and competencies.

Strengths or Assets	Weaknesses or Shortcomings
"I enjoy the morning paper. Thanks for bringing it in."	"Your hair is hanging in your eyes again."
	"How did you miss six? We went over the problems together".
	"I just swept the kitchen. Will you lean over!"
	"Don't complain about sitting in last chair. You never practice".

APPRECIATING RATHER THAN COMPARING

Parents can damage their child's self-esteem by comparing his skill levels to those of his sibling. Imagine for a moment that you are attending a ceramics class. You are happily chatting as you work on the ceramic rooster you are making for your Aunt Esther. You think it will make her feel good to think you spent all that time just because you cared about her.

Your teacher walks around the room and begins to

instruct, "Notice Mrs. Smith's gold paint. The flat appearance could have been improved by shading certain portions as Mrs. Jones has done." The instructor continues to compare the work of class members with the good intentions of helping her students improve their ceramics skills. As she draws closer to you, you suddenly don't feel so good about Aunt Esther's rooster. She raises your rooster for all to see, smiles politely and says, "It's very cute." Then she selects an identical rooster from the display case which a prize student has completed and suggests, "For a more realistic looking rooster, you could have blended the shades of brown and green together as this student has done."

While meaning to teach, this instructor has unintentionally made you feel you aren't as skillful in ceramics as you thought. You begin to doubt whether Aunt Esther will be thrilled over a "cute" rooster.

Sometimes parents with good intentions use this teaching technique with their children. They mean to help their children become more skillful by providing a model to copy. Often, however, they become killers of initiative, creative efforts, and feelings of self-worth instead.

Children naturally compare themselves to their brothers and sisters. Pointing out a sibling's expertise seldom helps a less skillful child become more proficient at a skill. Comparisons crush the child who feels insecure about his skills. Comparisons also harm the skillful child. The skillful child may temporarily feel good about the skill you recently compared to his less skillful sibling, but unconsciously may think, "I'm always being compared to my brother. I suppose I'm also being compared to Johnny next door and I know I'm not as good as he is."

Both children feel trapped. They see that their parents continually compare them to each other and to other children, and soon learn to compare themselves to other children in everything they do. They find little comfort in an occasional "comparison" victory, for they know that there is always someone out there who is better than they are at the same skill. Some children fold from the burden of unending comparisons, coming to the conclusion that they might as well not even try because they can never win the comparison game in the long run.

For example, John and Sylvia had their children very close together. It is quite obvious that their older child, Callie, is better at most skills than their younger daughter, Amanda. Callie is a better reader, a faster runner, further along in the piano book, more skillful at walking on stilts, plays ping pong better and usually wins in checkers against Amanda. How can they help Amanda feel she is skillful, competent and worthwhile?

John and Sylvia deal wisely with this difficult situation. They never compare the girls' skill levels in piano, reading, racing, and so on. Amanda, the younger, is aware that her older sister is more skillful than she in most areas, but this fact does not cause a serious problem for her because her parents apparently do not place much value on being better than someone else. John and Sylvia also do not use Callie as a model for improving Amanda's skills.

The girls' parents encourage the personal, *self-chosen* interests of each girl. Callie plays the cello, likes to sew and enjoys babysitting. Amanda plays the French horn, likes to draw and enjoys fishing. They have many personal interests which their parents use to point out their individual skills and competencies.

Callie and Amanda's parents praise their children without using comparison comments. They use what Haim Ginott calls *appreciative praise,* which tells the child how his behavior affects you and not how his behavior compares to some other standard (Ginott, 1965). For example, "I enjoy listening to you play that piece by Bach" or "Your work on the yard sure made it look better." Appreciative praise makes no comparison between one child's skillfullness and that of anyone else.

Both Callie and Amanda feel skillful, competent and worthwhile. They share a mutual respect and admiration for each other's interests and talents. Their wise parents never taught them how to play the "comparison game." As a result, they are both winners.

SKILL RECOGNITION CHECKLIST

The checklist below is intended to remind us of the importance of helping our children recognize their skills.

	Seldom	Some	Usually
1. I recognize my child's academic skills and point them out to him.			
2. I recognize my child's physical skills and point them out to him (riding a trike, swimming, basketball).			
3. I recognize my child's social skills and point them out to him (getting along with others, being kind, and considerate).			
4. I recognize the "little" skills and point them out to him (learning to whistle, mowing the grass, setting the table).			
5. I recognize my child's "non-academic" skill areas and point them out to him (carpentry, playing the guitar, repairing things).			
6. I think it is not important for my child to be more skillful than other children.			
7. I do not compare the skills of my child with his sibling's skills.			
8. I emphasize my child's skills rather than his shortcomings.			
9. I use "appreciative" praise rather than "comparison" praise.			
10. My child feels skillful, competent and rather worthwhile.			

Interpretation. If most of your checks are found in the "Usually" column, you are probably a parent who enhances his child's self-esteem by helping him to feel skillful, competent, and worthwhile. An abundance of checks in the "Seldom" column should act as a red flare, indicating that you may be delivering damaging messages to your child which make him feel inadequate and worthless.

chapter 12

Allowing Your Child to Grow at His Own Rate, in His Own Direction

From my back window I see and hear the beauty of spring, a season of growing. A mother robin fills her young's gaping mouth, waters of the stream rush into the pond, my five-year-old daughter giggles with a friend as they bury their feet in the cool sand, and the apple tree is covered with fragrant white blossoms which promise fruit in the months to come.

I think about the growing tree and the growing child. Shortly before the birth of our daughter, we planted an apple tree in our back yard. We fertilized it from time to time and protected it from bitter winters. Then we sat back patiently and allowed it to grow at its own rate, in its own way. We marvelled as it grew tall and straight, with such interesting branches. The fruit it bears is delicious. We might say the tree was "successful." It did what we wanted it to do.

During these five years, we have had faith in the seedling's ability to become a well-developed tree. We did not try to bend its limbs, overfertilize it, stunt its growth with too little water, or make it look like a maple instead of an apple tree. We simply planted it, provided nourishment and protection, and allowed it to grow.

A growing child needs to be nourished also, with many exciting living experiences to feed his mind and body. He needs to be protected from society's bitter elements until he is strong enough to face them alone. While providing quality nourishment and adequate protection, parents should sit back patiently and marvel as the child grows tall and straight, with such interesting personal characteristics. We should not push or manipulate the child, but allow him to become what he can be: a well-developed, successful adult who can experience fully the joys of life.

WHY DO PARENTS AND TEACHERS PUSH?

Parents who push and manipulate their child often do so with good intentions. They want them to turn out well and think they must prod and steer them through childhood in order to accomplish this.

For example, Kelly's mother is anxious for her daughter to grow into a successful adult but isn't sure how to help her. She watches her friends and neighbors as they provide for their children. If her neighbor's daughter enrolls in dancing classes, Kelly also is pushed into dancing lessons. When another neighbor fills out a form for summer gymnastics camp, Kelly's mother fills out a form also. A friend encourages her son's interest in art, buying him an easel and paints.

Although Kelly has never shown an interest in drawing, her mother gets her an easel and signs her up for art lessons. When Kelly doesn't show an interest in art, her mother is disappointed and thinks Kelly is lazy.

Kelly's mother pushes her daughter because she does not have faith in Kelly's ability to grow at her own rate, in her own direction. Because she isn't sure what helps a child grow to be a successful adult, she pushes Kelly into every possible "learning" experience. As a result, Kelly is so bombarded with things to do, she doesn't have time to discover her own interests and grow in the direction of her choice.

Another strong motive for pushing and manipulating children comes from a desire to prove, consciously or unconsciously, that we are good parents. We often believe that "good parents" produce children who can do everything expertly two years earlier than anyone else on the block. When a daughter is elected president of her class or wins an essay contest, we falsely see it as evidence of our skill as parents.

Pushy parents sometimes are adults who have not accomplished all they wanted to in their own lives. Now, instead of pursuing their own interests, they bask in the glory of their children's achievements, unconsciously reliving their own life through their children.

For some children the pushing begins at birth. A professor in a graduate education class spoke about research which indicated that pregnant mothers who engaged in prescribed pre-reading exercises during pregnancy delivered babies who read at a much earlier age. The research report was a hoax, and should have produced snickers from class members. "How wonderful," they thought, "now we can teach our children to read before they're born!"

The class reaction to the research spoof points to our society's obsession with pushing kids to perform at ever-increasing rates, never considering whether such remarkable early skills are beneficial to the child or are yet another way of robbing childhood from our children and never considering that children denied of a childhood do not become healthy, happy adults.

There is evidence of this pushing all around us. Children under the age of two are pushed to keep their panties dry through clever manipulations of sweet treats and ridiculous family celebrations. Pushy parents don't understand that most one and a half year olds don't have the physiological maturity for bladder control. They are convinced that their child will be smart enough to be toilet trained before age two.

Some nursery schools also push and manipulate children. Their classrooms are filled with impressive "teaching" devices designed to systematically teach a child everything he or she should know before entering "real" school. Research with young children, however, indicates that children learn in different ways. Such structured teaching devices cannot meet the needs of all individual children.

It is ironic that we systematically program the learning of a bright four-year-old with games and clever teaching toys from fear that he won't learn to read as well or as fast as we think he should. This same four-year-old, however, has just attained a very high degree of competency in the English language without structured teaching toys and structured teachers. He learned it, instead, by hearing and using language in its natural setting. Furthermore, he thoroughly enjoys the learning process and is delighted in his ability to communicate with others.

Books on how to teach your baby to read and raise his I.Q. 20 points fill the shelves of bookstores. Parents should ask, "Why should I teach my baby to read? I'm perfectly capable of reading to him, and we both enjoy it. Why should I attempt to raise his test score 20 points if raising his score has nothing to do with raising his innate intellectual potential?"

Early reading is sometimes seen by parents as the key to adult success. Enormous pressure is applied to preschools and kindergartens to put away the frivolous curriculum based on play and get on with the task of learning. All too often play is seen only as a useful tool to keep children busy while teachers work to push small groups of children through their numbers, letters, and colors.

THE IMPORTANCE OF PLAY

Fortunately, not all schools and parents accept this pressure cooker approach to assuring a child's future success in life. Recently, I overheard a mother helping a friend choose a nursery school for her three-year-old. She detailed the wonderful teaching toys in the school, the worksheets in prereading skills, the chart showing what each child knows and does not know. "My daughter has learned so much in her school. It is nothing like that 'other' school where all they do is play." The listening mother responded with much enthusiasm, asking, "Where is the school where all they do is play? It sounds like a place where my son can enjoy being a child without being pushed and manipulated."

This mother realizes the tremendous value of play in children's development, the unrushed setting it provides for children to grow and be totally absorbed in living right now. This mother wants her child to grow into a successful adult, and believes the best way to help her child achieve this goal is to provide experiences in which he can be a successful child. She does not want her son to compete with other three-year-olds, but to enjoy life now, becoming totally engrossed in learning through a natural play environment.

For some children the pushing continues throughout elementary school. The child spends 6½ hours in school, usually receiving carefully measured doses of spoon-fed learning. After school the child is chauffeured to dancing lessons, gymnastics class, piano lessons, choir practice, Little League practice, Boy Scout meetings and swimming lessons. After dinner there is supervised homework and practicing for each of the lessons. If everything runs according to the parent's schedule, the child may finish in time for bed. If not, he may be made to feel he didn't try hard enough or that he isn't very responsible.

Some children rebel against this lifestyle, refusing to practice or to fit into the schedule their parents have so carefully designed "for their own good." Other children submit to the regimentation of every waking minute with a weary resignation that "It must be good for me because my parents think so, but it sure isn't very much fun." Some children may think they enjoy this exhausting schedule which does not allow for reflection of inner growth. They continue this exhaustive schedule because they feel they must please their parents. These children may grow to be adults who have no time for quiet contemplation, no time to develop slow, comfortable relationships with people, no time to marvel over their own infant's sleepy yawn. After their parents stop pushing them, they continue to push themselves.

Adolescence is prime time for pushy parents, since it is their last chance to make sure their child "makes it." They prod their teenager to get better grades or to practice harder so he can star on the basketball team. They push him into dating even if he isn't interested, thinking he needs to develop dating skills for college.

All this pushing and manipulating sounds ridiculous, but under the heavy responsibilities of parenting, we sometimes catch ourselves directing the lives of our children. We must ask ourselves if we are helping them become the kind of persons *they choose* to become or placing roadblocks in their path by pushing them in the direction of our choice.

Childhood passes quickly. Parents should take time to enjoy their children as children. Don't rush them to be adults before they are ready. Allow them to have long, enriching childhoods with the knowledge that: "Enjoying childhood experiences to the fullest is the best preparation for becoming a mature adult" (LeShan, 1974, p. 324).

WHAT IS THE DIFFERENCE BETWEEN PUSHING AND ENCOURAGING?

Parents help their children acquire valued personal characteristics by encouraging desired behaviors, not by pushing behaviors.

Pushy parents make decisions about their child's life without consulting the child, as for example, "Here are your new tap shoes. You begin lessons Wednesday. You'll love it." They also bribe the child to move in the direction they choose for him, "If you read 25 books this summer, we will celebrate by going out to dinner." They give and take away love to manipulate the child: "Your father would be so proud if you went to medical school." They compare their child's skills with others in hopes of pushing the child toward success a little faster, "Your brother learned to ride a two-wheel bike when he was five."

In contrast, supportive and encouraging parents allow their child to discover new exciting things in life for himself. They give him the opportunity to make choices and decisions, and provide varied explorative experiences with no strings attached, from trips to the art museum to fishing jaunts. They support their child by showing an interest in his chosen activities—attending his baseball games, taking him to the library when he asks to go. If the child shows an interest in art, they ask him if he would like to take lessons and respect his decision. They let their child know what is available without pressuring him to participate.

The difference can be seen in the case of Mike and Roy, both skillful trumpet players in the high school band. When they were ten years old, the music director demonstrated the different kinds of instruments to the fifth graders. Both boys were very excited about the idea of playing an instrument in the band and confronted their parents with the idea.

Mike told his parents, "The trumpet is really neat. You get to play in the band and march at football games. Can I play the trumpet?" Mike's parents thought music might be something which he would enjoy, so they continued talking with Mike about his interest. They asked Mike how much a trumpet would cost. Mike found out the next day, and volunteered to work to pay for the horn. Mike practiced the trumpet only a few times a week, but worked very hard before concerts. Sometimes he forgot to take his horn to school, so he sat last chair for a while.

His parents told him when they noticed improvement in his tone quality. They attended his concerts and took a picture of Mike in his uniform which they framed and gave to him for Christmas. Mike organized four boys who practiced a piece for a contest and jammed together on weekends. When Mike grew up, he played trumpet in the community orchestra for enjoyment.

As a fifth grader, Roy told his parents, "This kid played the tuba and it sounded really neat. The director said they will need a tuba player next year, and he thinks I would be good at it. Can I play the tuba?" Roy's father agreed it would be a good experience to be in the band, but told Roy the tuba was too big and expensive. Roy found out that the school provides tubas to students, but his father had decided that the trumpet would be better because trumpets play melody and solo parts.

Soon after their discussion, Roy's parents gave him a new shiny trumpet, and signed him up for private lessons. His mother made sure Roy practiced every day and reminded him to take his horn to school every day so he wouldn't have to sit last chair. She pushed Roy into playing a solo at contest instead of joining Mike's quartet. Roy received a superior rating and was rewarded with a brand new, shinier trumpet. When Roy grew up, his trumpet remained at his parents' house in the attic.

HOW DOES PARENTAL PUSHING
AND MANIPULATION AFFECT THE
CHILD'S SELF-CONCEPT?

The child who is continually pushed and manipulated cannot develop a strong, positive self-concept. When his parents direct his every move, they send damaging messages to him which say, "You are not capable of making decisions on your own, so I make them for you. You are lazy, so I must push you. You don't have the ability to grow into a successful adult by your own initiative, so I must push you in the right direction." These messages make the child feel lazy and incompetent. When the child feels that way, he will act that way. With low self-esteem, he will have little interest or enthusiasm for trying new behaviors, because he is afraid that he will not succeed.

Parents who *support* and *encourage* their child's interests and endeavors rather than pushing and manipulating the child's life send helpful messages which say, "You are capable of making wise decisions about your life. You have the ability to grow into a successful adult by your own initiative." These messages help the child develop a strong, positive self-concept. He feels ambitious, competent, and worthwhile, and will be able to greet life with interest and enthusiasm.

ENCOURAGING VERSUS PUSHING CHECKLIST
The checklist below can offer parents a general idea of where they stand in terms of pushing and manipulating, or supporting and encouraging their children.

	Seldom	Some	Usually
1. I provide my child with many explorative experiences with no strings attached.			
2. I allow and encourage my child to find and try new experiences.			

	Seldom	Some	Usually
3. I listen attentively (without judging) to my child's excitement over things which are of interest to him and make him happy.			
4. I have a good idea of what things in life bring my child joy, because I listen to him.			
5. I support and encourage my child's interests by asking if I can be of any help to him.			
6. I support all "constructive" interests my child has, even though I might not find those areas enjoyable.			
7. I select schools and teachers for my child which allow him to grow at his own rate, in his own direction.			
8. I enroll my child in lessons without consulting him about his desire to participate.			
9. I think that parents are in a better position to know what might be enjoyable for their child. Children aren't really old enough to know.			
10. I respond to my child's excitement over his interests by pointing out those things which are more worthwhile than others.			
11. I don't really know what my child enjoys but he doesn't either, so I lead him to the good things in life.			
12. I encourage my child's interests if I value them; otherwise, I ignore them and hope they go away.			
13. I let my child make decisions about his life but help him to make the right ones.			
14. I select schools and teachers for my child which will push and manipulate him so he will "look good" when he is an adult.			

Intepretation: Checks in the third column on statements 1–7 and checks in the first column on statements 8–14 indicate you probably are a parent who allows and encourages your child to grow at his own rate, in his own "constructive" direction. Checks in the first column on statements 1–7 and checks in the third column on statements 8–14 indicate you may be a parent who is afraid your child can't live his life well by himself, and is pushing him in the "right" direction.

Every child wants to grow up to be free, to be totally himself. A bright six-year-old expressed this desire when she asked her pushing mother, "Why can't you let me be how I grow?" (LeShan, 1974).

WISHES FOR YOUR CHILDREN

All parents want their children to be successful and most are willing to help their children attain that goal. However, our definitions of success vary. We might view the successful person as one who makes a lot of money, lives in the right neighborhood, and has a college diploma hanging in the den. However, most of us have also known the man or woman who wallows in material possessions, has several diplomas, and is still unhappy. We would be wise to stop for a moment and think seriously about what we really want for our children. Does the destination we visualize for our children include something more than money and status? What is our idea of a successful person, one who has turned out well?

The strategy which follows, "Wishes for My Child," gives you an opportunity to clarify your thinking about what is important for your children. Once you have a clear picture of what you want for your children, you may better help them become what they can—well-developed, happy, successful adults who can experience fully the joys of being alive.

WISHES FOR MY CHILD

Wishes for My Child (Part one): If you were able to make wishes come true, what characteristics would you wish your child to possess when he becomes an adult? On the page below, write fifteen wishes or more for your child, characteristics for him to possess as an adult. Write anything that comes to your mind, both big and small qualities. For now, disregard the squares and circles before the numbers.

○ ☐ 1.

○ ☐ 2.

○ ☐ 3.

○ ☐ 4.

○ ☐ 5.

○ ☐ 6.

○ ☐ 7.

○ ☐ 8.

○ ☐ 9.

○ ☐ 10.

○ ☐ 11.

○ ☐ 12.

○ ☐ 13.

○ ☐ 14.

○ ☐ 15.

If you are working on this strategy with another person, a wife, husband, or friend, discuss your wishes with each other after you finish your list. If there is a wish on their list you think is important, add it to your list. No two lists will be exactly the same because no two people have identical values. There are no "right" or "wrong" values.

Wishes for My Child (Part two):   Using the wish list above, rank each item in the *square* provided according to the importance you attach to it. Some items will be difficult to rank because they overlap to some degree. The specific rank for any one item is not important. The overall picture of where the wishes fall in the ranking is desired. Is the characteristic a high-priority item, or does it fall near the bottom of the list?

Wishes for My Child (Part three):   Using the wish list above, mark each item in the *circle* provided with one of three codes. Mark a ($) if the item depends primarily on money. Use an (S) if the item depends heavily on having status. Mark an (FS) if the attainment of this item depends heavily on feelings about one's self. Some items may need two codes, but most can be coded with only one symbol.

Several groups of parents have worked on "Wishes for My Child." A composite list follows. The asterisk identifies items which were consistently found near the top of most lists. What similarities and differences do you find between your list and the composite list of this group of parents?

Parents' Composite Wish List

*be a responsible person
*have meaningful work
*be emotionally stable
*have a good self-concept
*have meaningful relationships with others
*be happy
*enjoy life
*be healthy

*have enough money
  have a special talent
  have good feelings about one's body
  know one's roots (heritage)
  be a law-abiding citizen
  have an optimistic attitude
  have musical ability
  have children
  have self-confidence
  be intelligent
  have agility in sports
  like his or her parents
  have morals
  be resourceful
  be humble
  have a large vocabulary
  have a sense of humor
  be sincere
  have a continuing desire to learn
  be a religious person
  be unselfish
  live near parents
  be independent
  have determination and drive
  be able to give happiness to others
  have a deep, loving relationship with a spouse

It is interesting to note that the highest priority wishes (marked with *) have little to do with wealth or status. One item does say "have enough money," but emphasis is placed on the enough instead of a lot.

When parents take time to seriously think about what they want for their children they don't list, "make a lot of money, live in the right neighborhood, and have a college diploma hanging in the den." Rather, they seem to value being responsible, productive physically and mentally healthy, able to maintain meaningful relationships with others, and having a positive self-concept.

How Can I Help My Child
Attain These Wishes?

Having worked through the "Wishes for My Child," you probably have a clearer picture of what characteristics you wish your child to possess when he becomes an adult. Unfortunately we can't grant wishes for our children. One of the most effective ways to help a child attain certain attributes as an adult is to help him or her possess those attributes as a child. We often think too much about preparing the child for tomorrow. The most important factor which determines how the child lives tomorrow is how he lives today.

Wish. "I want my child to enjoy life when he is an adult." If we want our child to enjoy life as an adult, we must make sure he learns how to enjoy life today. We must allow and encourage the child to discover and choose those things in life which bring him joy, and we cannot always predict what that will be. While we may enjoy piano, this may not be a source of joy for your child. The child who is overscheduled won't find much joy in living today, and no number of wonderful skills will guarantee that he will enjoy life as an adult. The child who is allowed the opportunity to watch mallards on the pond caring for their ducklings will enjoy the wonders of nature and life as a child. When he becomes an adult, he will be able to enjoy his own young child and, again, marvel at nature and life. **To be good at enjoying life as an adult, the child needs to practice enjoying life today.**

Wish. "I want my child to be a responsible person when he is an adult." If we want our child to be a responsible adult, we must allow and encourage him to be responsible now. If we make all the decisions about his life today, we deny him the opportunity to learn how to make decisions on his own and learn to be responsible for his own actions. The child needs to make many decisions, although some will surely be unwise. He can learn from both good and bad decisions, but cannot learn from making no decisions. **To be a responsible adult, the child needs to practice learning how to be responsible today.**

Wish. "I want my child to be a productive adult." If we want our child to become a productive adult we must allow and encourage him to be productive as a child. Today the child can be productive by painting a picture in nursery school, raking the front lawn, or being a life guard at the beach. Tomorrow he can be productive farming 500 acres, teaching math in the high school, or doing volunteer work at the hospital. **To be productive as an adult, the child needs to practice being productive today.**

Wish. "I want my child to have meaningful relationships with others when he is an adult." If we want our child to have meaningful realtionships with others as an adult, we must allow and encourage him to develop meaningful realtionships with others today. This begins at the moment of birth, when the mother establishes the absolutely essential bond with her child; the child's first and most important relationship with another person. Quality relationships with other family members help the child develop meaningful relationships with people outside his family—friends, peers, spouse. Children who do not experience loving relationships with others as a child cannot develop loving relationships with others as an adult. **To be able to have meaningful relationships with others as an adult, the child needs to practice developing meaningful relationships with others today.**

Wish. "I want my child to be happy when he is an adult." If we want our child to be happy as an adult, we must allow and encourage him to be happy today. Laugh with your child and do silly, spontaneous, fun things. Sometimes parents become too serious. Good, responsible parents can smile, laugh, and enjoy life. **To be happy as an adult, the child needs to practice being happy today.**

Practice *does* make perfect in the wishes we have for our children as adults. **The more practice a child gets today at being happy, responsible and productive, having good feelings about himself, and developing meaningful relationships with others, the better chance he will have to possess those same characteristics tomorrow as an adult.**

chapter 13

Having Realistic Expectations for Your Child

Father, peering through the nursery window at his new son, is filled with great joy. Undoubtedly, his head is full of many thoughts about his son and what they will share in the years to come. What expectations does this father have for his son? One father who is waving a football in front of the window may have expectations concerning the *relationship* he dreams will grow between his son and him; one built on warmth, sharing, and love. He imagines what it will be like sharing days with this wonderful child, tucking him in bed at night, tossing the football back and forth, understanding his joy and pain, and living a relationship based on love.

Another football-waving father may have a very different set of expectations for his infant son. The football may symbolize all the remarkable *achievements* he expects his son

to attain in the future. This father imagines the joy he will feel when he sees his son racing his motorcycle with extraordinary skill and daring, when his son is elected president of his class, or when he wins a football scholarship to a prestigious college.

The football symbolizes two different sets of expectations. One concerns the relationship between a parent and child; the other concerns the child's achievement in areas which are important to the parent.

HOW PARENTAL EXPECTATIONS AFFECT CHILDREN'S SELF-CONCEPTS

It is natural for parents to want their children to be competent and successful in life. However, we may become overly ambitious for our children and place too much emphasis on their achievements. We begin to forget about the child himself and our relationship with him. Unintentionally we may develop unrealistic expectations for him and begin to pressure him to meet those expectations.

The parent who narrowly focuses on achievement teaches his child to focus on achievement also. The child then senses that his worth is determined by how much he achieves, and drives himself to achieve so that he can gain his parents' approval and love. If the child does not meet his parents' expectations, he feels incompetent, worthless, and unlovable. These feelings are the basis of a negative self-concept.

In contrast, parents who focus on developing a supportive, loving relationship with their child provide a safe, nourishing environment in which the child can grow. The child feels he is loved "just because he is" and doesn't struggle to win his parents' love through achievements. He develops good feelings about himself which give him the freedom and motivation to set his own expectations and achieve his own goals.

WHERE DO UNREALISTIC EXPECTATIONS COME FROM?

Most parents have a general idea of the steps through which children progress during their growing years, and childcare books offer charts stating the average age at which children accomplish various feats. The one-year-old learns to walk. The two- to three-year-old becomes toilet trained. At four he dresses himself. At six he ties his shoes.

There is nothing wrong with charts giving information about the growth and development of children. It is what parents do with the information which causes difficulties for the child. Some parents, fearing their child might fall behind, place too much emphasis on keeping up with the averages on the growth chart. They form expectations for their child based on averages, which may be unrealistic for their own child who has a personal timetable directing his unique growth.

Parents may panic when they notice a neighbor's five-year-old riding a two-wheel bike while their own six-year-old is still content to ride a tricycle. They observe their ten-year-old niece placing her napkin on her lap before eating while their own twelve-year-old son ignores his folded napkin throughout the entire meal. Suddenly, riding two-wheel bikes and learning table manners become expectations for their children.

Unrealistic expectations for children also come from parents who don't have good feelings about themselves. Parents who feel they have not accomplished all they wanted in life, often decide the same thing isn't going to happen to their child. They are going to do everything they can to make sure their child achieves. These parents set expectations which are unrealistic for their children and pressure them to meet those expectations.

WHAT HAPPENS TO THE CHILD WHOSE PARENTS HAVE UNREALISTIC EXPECTATIONS FOR HIM?

When parents develop demanding and unrealistic achievement expectations for their child, the child may fail to meet those expectations. When he does fail, the parent becomes disappointed or even angry. He may think the child is just being stubborn and isn't really trying to achieve. The face and words of the disappointed or angry parent clearly informs the child that he has not measured up to the parent's expectations. The child, in turn, becomes disappointed in

PARENTAL EXPECTATIONS:	CHILD FAILS:	CHILD FEELS:	CHILD SEES HIMSELF AS:
Child should make the baseball team as Dad did when he was an eight-year-old.	Child doesn't make the team and really likes tennis better.	"I let my Dad down. He thinks less of me now."	Not good in sports: a failure.
Child should get all A's in school because he has a high I.Q.	Child doesn't get all A's and spends more time playing with friends than studying.	"I have failed in my parents' eyes."	Lazy and not worthwhile.
Three-year-old child should be able to put all his toys away.	Child picks up a few toys, but then cries.	"My mom is mad at me. She doesn't love me 'cause I don't pick up my toys."	A bad person.

himself. He thinks, "I'm not skillful. I'm a person who fails." His self-esteem decreases.

Even if the child pushes himself to perform unrealistic tasks set by his parents, he still *feels* like a failure because he knows he has accomplished those tasks due to his parents' efforts (pushing) rather than because of his own initiative. He does not feel successful unless he himself is motivated to complete tasks. He concludes: "I made the baseball team just like Dad wanted, but I still don't like baseball. It may make my dad feel good that I'm on the team, but it doesn't make me feel good. I don't like the things he thinks I should like. I know I'm a disappointment to my dad."

DOES THIS MEAN PARENTS SHOULDN'T HAVE ANY EXPECTATIONS FOR THEIR CHILDREN?

If unrealistic expectations cause children to feel inadequate and worthless, should parents have no expectations for their children? No. The child whose parents have no expectations for him leave the child alone to flounder and find his own way. Parents should encourage growth in their child and share his joy in accomplishments. A lack of any parental expectations may lead to the feeling that the parents don't care if the child succeeds, again causing children to develop negative self-concepts. Providing learning opportunities for children which encourage them to take new steps is desirable, as long as the expectations are realistic.

WHAT ARE REALISTIC EXPECTATIONS FOR CHILDREN?

Realistic expectations are based on the individual child and his readiness to take steps forward. When assessing the readiness of our child to take that next step, we should consider a few factors which are characteristic of the growth and development of children.

Children are born with different characteristics and potentials. Probably only one child among thousands is born with the potential to become a virtuoso pianist. The remaining children may become fine pianists, but it would be unrealistic and harmful for their parents to expect them to reach virtuoso status.

Children grow at different rates. Children do not make steady, even progress in all areas of development. They may reach a plateau in one area and spurt in another. Children often seem to need a rest after big jumps in development. This uneven growth is normal. Parents must wait patiently for the next surge in growth without pushing unrealistic expectations on the child.

Growing children take steps backward as well as forward. We rejoice when our children take forward steps. It is also normal for children to take backward steps when they find their latest forward step is uncomfortable. For example, five-year-old Jason concerned his parents by his "unexplainable" behaviors. His father explains. "We just don't understand Jason's behavior lately. He balks at everything we ask him to do. When we ask him to do something we know he can do, he says he can't. This summer we enrolled him in swimming lessons. He can dive off the board, but refused to do so when we asked him to. When the teacher forced him to dive, he did. The next lesson he cried and refused to dive again. Also, we taught him to tie his shoes a few months ago. Now he won't do it and says he can't. We're worried because he seems to be regressing rather than moving ahead."

Jason's parents have set unrealistic expectations for him. Although Jason does have the physical and mental ability necessary to dive off the board and tie his shoes, Jason is not emotionally ready to perform these skills. Initially, Jason took the forward step by learning to tie his shoes and dive from the board. Feeling uncomfortable at this level of accomplishment, he decided to step backward awhile. Jason should be allowed to take a step backward, and remain there until *he feels* ready to move forward again. He should not be pressured by his parents with, "You did it before, I know you can do it now." Pressure of this kind will have negative effects on Jason's self-concept, and the more negative his self-concept, the less ready he will be to take forward steps of any kind. Prodding and pushing only slow growth.

We cannot know for sure why Jason took the backward step. Perhaps he tried diving and it was frightening. Maybe he is afraid his demanding swimming teacher will make him do other, more difficult things in the water which he won't like. Jason may have decided not to tie his shoes because it is hard for him and they always come untied later. Or perhaps he prefers to have his mother tie his shoes because this makes him feel like she cares about him and wants to help him. At this time in Jason's life he may not be sure he wants to be "a bigger boy." He thinks he prefers the stage he is in right now and wants to wait before taking another forward step.

In determining *realistic* expectations for a child, the parent needs to be sensitive to the physical, mental, and emotional readiness of the child to take that next forward step. Parents need to ask themselves, "Does my child really want to take the next step, or is it I, the parent, who is ready for him to take the step?"

HOW CAN YOU KNOW WHEN YOUR CHILD IS READY TO TAKE A FORWARD STEP?

Children are usually the best judges of their readiness to try new things. Parents need to expose them to new and exciting living experiences, sit back, and then patiently wait for them to give us signs that they are ready to move ahead. For example, children observe people tying their shoes all the time. Someday your child will show an interest in learning how to tie his own shoes, perhaps coming home from kindergarten announcing, "Teddy can tie his shoes so he doesn't have to wait for the teacher to do it. He always gets to be first out for recess. I want to learn how to tie my shoes so I can be first, too." Or you simply find him curled up on the couch fiddling with his shoe strings one day, trying to figure out how it's done. These are the signs which tell the parent that his child is probably ready to take a step forward.

Realistic expectations for a child are those which help him grow to be happy and feel competent. It is important that your child knows he is pleasing you and that you are proud of the way he is growing and developing at his own pace. The child who has many successful experiences in meeting realistic expectations develops good feelings about himself. He feels competent and enthusiastically meets new challenges because he is confident he can succeed. The child who does not often experience success and fails to meet his parents' unrealistic expectations grows to believe he will fail everything he attempts because he has failed so often in the past.

Some parents mistakenly believe that if they push their child to do something hard and he succeeds, he will feel like he has accomplished something. Instead, the child who has been pushed to accomplish something he was not ready to face may conclude, "It's hard to succeed. I only accomplish things when my parents are there to push me. I'm not really a very capable person or it would not be such a struggle for me to succeed." This child may also believe that his parents don't approve of him since they don't accept his opinion concerning when he should attempt new tasks.

chapter 14

Developing a Quality Relationship with Your Child

On graduation day, Marian and Ted sit in the audience watching their son march by to receive his diploma. They are proud of their son's academic achievements, athletic awards, his tall stature and his straight teeth.

On this day they are finally able to relax—no more pressure to make sure he grows up right. Yet, something seems to be missing. A sad realization comes to them—they don't *really* know the boy walking across the stage.

Marian and Ted have been so busy these past eighteen years "molding" their son that they have forgotten to take time to enjoy him, to see him as a beautiful, special human being. They have not allowed themselves to share his joys, disappointments, and excitement with life. The relationship they have developed with their son is little more than a

surface one. Dutifully, they have chauffeured him to the orthodontist, replaced his worn out tennis shoes, and made sure he ate two leafy, green vegetables each day. They have met their son's physical needs but have done little to nourish him emotionally. A child's emotional needs can be met only through a quality parent-child relationship: a relationship which considers inside needs as well as outside needs.

WHAT IS A QUALITY RELATIONSHIP?

A quality parent-child relationship is one which nurtures the child's self-concept, allowing him to feel loved and worthwhile. The relationship gives parents the opportunity to deliver messages to the child which say: "I enjoy being with you. You are special and important. I care very much about you and want to share your joys, fears, disappointments, and dreams." This kind of relationship helps the child feel good about himself and allows him to grow strong, emotionally.

The development of a quality parent-child relationship has three major requirements:

1. that parents know their child well;
2. that parents give their child focused attention;
3. that parents accept and cherish their child.

KNOWING YOUR CHILD

Do you know the condition of your child's tennis shoes? How soon before he needs another haircut? When was his last dental checkup? What is his favorite shirt? Parents can answer these questions easily by observing what is going on "outside" of the child. The need to replace moldy tennis shoes or retrieve a certain shirt after six continuous days of wearing is quite obvious to parents.

Not so obvious is what our child looks like on the "inside." How does our child feel about the world around him? What are his most recent disappointments? What does he enjoy most in life? What is his favorite family activity? These questions are more difficult to answer because they deal with feelings which come from within the child. A quality relationship depends on parents knowing what their child feels on the "inside" as well as on the child knowing how the parent feels on the "inside."

Strategy—"Getting to Know You"

The object of this strategy is to learn more about family members and yourself, to discover what makes people in your family happy, and to find out what makes each family member special. Sitting together, listening to others, and offering positive feedback help members of the family feel better about themselves. The process strengthens family bonds.

Directions: Family members sit in a circle or around a table (maybe at meal time). Taking turns, each family member completes the first sentence. "I get a lot of pleasure when I . . . . . .", someone might add "when I march in the football games" or "when I prepare dinner for friends." All sentences must be completed with positive endings. Some questions may need to be reworded for young children. Comments concerning another person's answers must be supportive and positive. The purpose of this strategy is to help people we care about feel good about themselves. Warm, supportive comments are encouraged, for they are the messages which help people grow toward increased self-esteem.

Sentence stems:

1.   I get a lot of pleasure when I . . . .
2.   If I could spend all my time at school in one class, it would be . . . .
3.   I am happiest with myself when I . . . .
4.   Something I can do now that I couldn't do a few years ago is . . . .
5.   My father makes me feel good when he says . . . .
6.   My mother makes me feel good when she says . . . .
7.   One thing I'm good at is . . . .
8.   My parents think I am good at . . . .
9.   When I was younger, I liked to . . . .
10. The one thing I most want to accomplish is . . . .
11. (For children) When I grow up I might like to be _____ or _____ .

     (for parents) If I didn't have my present job I might like to _____ or _____ .
12. My teachers think ("used to think" for parents) I am (was) good at . . . .
13. At home my three favorite things to do alone are . . . .

14.   I am proud that I . . . .
15.   At home my three favorite things to do with the
      family are . . . .
16.   Three words which describe me pretty well are
      . . . . .
17.   Three words which describe my mother are
      . . . .
18.   Three words which describe my dad are . . . .
19.   (For parents) Three words that describe my son or
      daughter are . . . .
20.   The thing I like best about myself is
      . . . .

GIVING YOUR CHILD FOCUSED ATTENTION

The development of a quality parent-child relationship requires that parents give their child "focused attention." For most of us, the days and weeks whisk by quickly. We find ourselves swept along in the hectic pace of modern-day living, and focus our attention on the pure logistics of getting through each day: packing lunch boxes, baking brownies for the hospital bake sale, mowing the lawn, and washing the car may be attended to today while quality time spent with our child is put off until tomorrow. By evening we are sometimes mentally and physically drained, unable to tune in to our child's life. If we are not careful, the pushes and pulls of daily living monopolize our energy and attention and cause us to drift away from our child.

Young children are usually very persistent in trying to gain their parents' attention. They beg, "Play with me, Mommy. Daddy, please read me a book." If these simple requests are ignored, they persist with more shocking and irritating methods of gaining attention. They become whiners, they violently rock the parent's chair as he tries to read the newspaper, they antagonize their siblings until they cry, they write on walls with crayons. They try anything they think might get their parents to stop what they are doing and pay attention to them. These children are sending the message, "I need you! I need you to pay attention to me. I need you to show me you care about me."

If the child's efforts to gain his parents' attention prove futile, he eventually gives up trying and drifts further away from his parents' life. When we fail to respond to our child's thoughts and feelings, he is forced to carry on with life by himself. A child who is tuned out day after day sadly concludes: "I'm not very important or special to my parents. They don't seem to enjoy being with me, probably because I'm not really very worthwhile or lovable." The parent-child relationship deteriorates when the child is continually put off and deprived of his parents' attention and the child's self-concept suffers markedly.

The kind of attention children receive from their parents is important. Some kinds of attention deliver harmful messages to children and cause them to develop negative feelings about themselves.

Substitute attention, for example, keeps the parents at a distance from their child's life while attempting to pacify the

Substitute Attention tells the child, "I don't have time for you but here is a pacifier to take my place."

child with diversions. This attention substitutes "things" and "activities" for the parent.

The boy in the drawing needs something much more important than the kite he received: he wants his father to give something of himself. His father, however, does not share his son's life and suggests instead that his son get his attention from a kite or a neighbor. Repeated material pacifiers force the child to conclude that he is not important enough or loved enough to warrant his parents' time and attention. Substitute attention does not nurture a quality parent-child relationship.

Negative attention also harms rather than helps the parent-child relationship. For example, Barbara prided herself with the fact that she stayed home with her children all through their school years. Yet, she regretfully felt that she did not have a very good relationship with them. Although Barbara was with her children during their every waking hour, she still did not provide the kind of attention they needed. Parents and children must share more than physical space with each other to develop a quality relationship: They must share themselves.

Negative Attention tells the child, "You are a nuisance and I don't enjoy having you around."

In the drawing we see a father sharing physical space with his child. Father does pay attention to his daughter. He notices his daughter's activities and expresses his feelings about those activities. However, the kind of attention he gives is very damaging, because it is negative. The daughter hears the negative messages loud and clear, "You're a nuisance. You're a trouble maker. I don't enjoy being with you." Father's messages help the child to conclude that she is incompetent, worthless, and unlovable. Negative attention damages the parent-child relationship.

Sometimes parents give their child *pretend attention.* When engrossed in their own personal thoughts or activities, they pretend to be interested in what is happening in their child's life. For instance, the parent in the drawing is really absorbed in a television program, but pretends to give her child attention. Children are not fooled by pretend attention. They know their parents are not really paying attention to what they are doing at the moment. If parents continually give pretend attention, the child will eventually conclude,

Pretend Attention tells the child, "What is on T.V. is more important and interesting than what goes on in your life."

"What goes on in my world is not very important or interesting to Mom and Dad." Pretend attention does not foster a quality parent-child relationship. Attention which nourishes the parent-child relationship must be *focused attention*. Focused attention includes listening and responding to the child with all our senses. We see what the child is doing, we hear what he or she is saying, we empathize with his feelings, and we share completely that moment of his life. For example, the parent in the drawing is completely tuned in to her child during their brief encounter. She looks at his drawings and seriously thinks about what she sees. She allows herself to marvel at her child's ability to "make flowers look like they are waving." The child *knows* his mother is sincerely interested in his work and feels good about sharing this moment of his life with her. Their relationship is enhanced by this moment of focused attention.

This does not mean that parents must spend every moment of their life in focused attention on their child. In this drawing for, example, Father is mowing the lawn. His

Focused Attention tells the child, "You do good work. What you do in your life is very interesting to me."

Delayed Attention tells the child, "I'm in the middle of something now, but I *do* want to be with you when I finish."

son requests his father's attention. Although he assures his son that he is interested in the things he does and wants to see what he has been doing, Father does not quit his task to provide focused attention to his child. Instead, he explains that his attention will be delayed temporarily. It is important in this parent-child encounter that Father does attend to his child when he finishes the task at hand. The delay in focused attention does not harm the child, because the child knows his father is interested in him and will soon give him focused attention.

Children differ in the amount of focused time they need with their parents. There are times in the child's life when he needs more focused attention than other times such as when a new baby arrives home or when there is other additional stress in the family. Children need additional quality, focused attention from their parents when their environment causes them to feel insecure about themselves as worthwhile and lovable human beings. It is not possible or necessary to give our children focused attention every minute of every day. What is necessary is that we give them enough quality attention to feel securely loved and worthwhile.

ACCEPTING AND CHERISHING
YOUR CHILD

A fifth-grade teacher once asked her students to complete unfinished sentences as an English assignment. One stem sentence read, "A parent is someone who . . . ." The children's responses varied. However, one theme was found in several children's answers, "A parent is someone who tells you everything you do wrong so you can grow up right."

In an effort to help our children "grow up right" we sometimes concentrate too heavily on pointing out to them all the areas in which they need to improve: "Tuck in your shirt so you won't look so sloppy. . . . That was a selfish thing for you to do. . . . Again, you did not clean your plate." We justify these negative comments by saying to our child, "I'm telling you this for your own good so you can learn and grow into a better person," and by calling our comments "constructive criticism." Children seldom benefit when we find fault with them, pick at their errors, point out their weaknesses, criticize their thoughts and behaviors, reject their way of living, and show our non-acceptance of them. Criticism seldom helps a child grow into a better person. Instead, it makes it more difficult for them to grow in positive directions.

Put yourself in the child's place for a moment. Your spouse has just put his arm around you and said, "Honey, I have some constructive criticism to give to you, for your own good. I'm not rejecting you personally, but only trying to help you change your behavior. Honey, you are a slob. You leave your clothes laying all over the bedroom and you're getting fat as a pig." How would you feel after hearing this well-meaning constructive criticism? Do you get much satisfaction knowing your spouse rejects your "behavior" and not you personally, or do you find it difficult to differentiate the two kinds of rejection?

We sometimes attempt to defend constructive criticism by thinking, "I'm not rejecting or disapproving of my child as a person, only of his behavior." We may be able to understand this distinction, but children have difficulty telling the difference between a parent's rejection of him as a person and their rejection of his behavior. Regardless of the intent, constructive criticism damages the child's self-esteem. What the child needs to "grow up right" is acceptance and unconditional love.

Accepting the child also means accepting the way he lives and grows. Children need their parents to accept and cherish their uniqueness and their personal way of living. For example, one day after dinner six-year-old Carrie asked, "Daddy, will you play with me?" Father replies, "Yes, I would like to play with you. I'll rest for ten minutes and then we will play together. You be deciding what we will play." After ten minutes, Carrie led her father to the family room to begin their play. To Father's surprise, he was instructed to crawl under the ping pong table in near darkness, where awaited an array of puzzles for them to complete.

Carrie's father's own "adult needs" dictated that puzzles should be worked while sitting in an easy chair, certainly not sprawled under some table with barely enough light to see the pieces. However, he considers "Carrie's need" to share her world as she creates it with someone who cares about her and spends half an hour under the table putting puzzles together.

Later, when they crawled from beneath the table, both were glowing from the caring and sharing they experienced together. Carrie's father's acceptance of her world and ways made her feel good to be herself. Carrie and her father have a relationship which nourishes a positive self-concept. When the parent accepts and loves the child as a unique human being, the child accepts and loves himself and develops a positive self-concept.

One summer my ten-year-old daughter, Cathy, and her friend, Stephanie, decided to decorate the playhouse. When finished, they were covered from head to toe with brown stain and yellow paint. I could not resist taking a picture of the two of them in a "We're pals" embrace. Cathy framed the picture, wrote a caption at the bottom, and gave it to her friend. The caption read, "A friend is someone who loves you even when you're dirty." Parents who desire a quality relationship with their child would do well to adopt similar words of wisdom: A parent is someone who loves and accepts you even when you're dirty, forgetful, rude, clumsy and imperfect in so many ways.

QUALITY ATTENTION CHECKLIST

The checklist below is intended to remind us of the importance of providing our children with quality attention.

		Seldom	Some	Usually
1.	Even though I am a busy person, I make time to provide quality attention for my child.			
2.	I am *with* my child enough, but I still don't feel I know him very well.			
3.	I give my child "focused" attention, tuning in completely to what he is saying, doing and feeling.			
4.	I am so busy making sure my child grows up right I find it hard to simply enjoy him as a special, beautiful human being.			
5.	When I must be temporarily unavailable to my child I assure him that I want to be with him. Then, I *soon* make the time to be with him.			
6.	My life is so hectic that I find I am too tired to be able to give "focused" attention to my child.			
7.	The kind of attention I give my child tells him, "Your life is very important to me."			
8.	I give my child "substitute" attention (material items, outside activities) to make up for my inability to give him "quality" attention.			

	Seldom	Some	Usually
9. I love and accept my child even when he is dirty, forgetful, rude, clumsy, and imperfect in so many ways.			
10. The kind of attention I give my child tells him, "You are a nuisance and I don't really enjoy having you under my feet."			

If you responded to these statements with checks in the "Usually" column for odd-numbered statements and checks in the "Seldom" column for even-numbered statements, you are probably a parent who has developed a quality relationship with his child.

chapter 15

Listening and Responding with Empathy to Your Child's Feelings

Remember what it was like being a child, struggling to grow up? There was the humiliation you felt when your mother insisted you wear black boots to school, the embarrassment of your face being dotted with pimples, and the pain of being excluded from the "in-group." As children the problems were very serious to us. As adults we can smile when we recall how earthshaking they seemed at the time. When we see our own children experiencing many of the same painful feelings of disappointment, rejection, fear, anger, we wish we could help them through their growing years.

We *can* help our children deal with the problems of growing in three ways: 1) by *being there* when they need someone to talk with; 2) by *understanding and caring* about their experiences and feelings; 3) and by *accepting and encouraging* their efforts to deal with their problems and feelings. When we show children that we understand and care about their feelings and believe in their ability to handle them effectively, we support their growing.

The key to understanding our children's feelings is good listening. The way we listen and respond to them greatly affects the way they feel about themselves. Listening and responding with empathy, caring, and patience, helps them feel competent, worthwhile and lovable. Listening and responding with criticism, sarcasm, and rejection encourages them to feel incompetent, worthless, and unlovable. We can develop a close, meaningful, and helpful relationship with our child by listening and responding to him or her in constructive ways.

WHAT MAKES PARENTS GOOD LISTENERS?

A parent is a helpful listener when he or she:

1. encourages the child to express his or her feelings openly;
2. takes the child's feelings seriously;
3. listens between the lines for the hidden messages the child delivers;
4. listens and responds without critical judgments, put-downs, or lectures;
5. tries to understand what the child is feeling.

Encourage the Child to Express His Feelings Openly

How the child feels at any moment is the result of what is happening around and to him. The child often has a need to share his feelings with another person, someone who loves and cares about him. Parents often fill this role.

Parents who do not listen carefully or who hastily respond with criticism to their child's feelings discourage the child from sharing his feelings. The child may interpret this to mean there is something wrong with his feelings or with him as a person. In contrast, parents who listen attentively to what their child says and respond with empathy and understanding encourage this kind of sharing and help their child believe that his feelings are important, that he is important as a person.

In the following conversation, eleven-year-old Rhonda expresses her embarrassment and anger at an incident which occurred in school. What kind of listener is Rhonda's mother?

MOTHER: (Noticing the slighted chores and Rhonda's troubled looking face) It looks like something is bothering you.

RHONDA: It sure is. You'd be bothered too if your best friend, or at least you thought your best friend, did what she did to me.

MOTHER: Sharon made you angry?

RHONDA: I hate her. I'll never speak to her again. You won't believe what she did, Mom. Between classes, she gave a note to Eric that said, 'Dear Eric, I'm madly in love with you. I can't live without you. Love, Rhonda.' Some kids found the note and read it in front of everyone. And I didn't write the stupid note. Sharon said it was only a joke. Some joke. All the kids laughed at me.

MOTHER: I can understand why you are upset. It must have been embarrassing when everyone heard the note and thought you wrote it.

RHONDA: It sure was. I'm so mad and it's all Sharon's fault.

MOTHER: What Sharon thought would be a joke turned out to hurt you. It is hard when your best friend hurts you.

RHONDA: (Pauses to think) I don't think she meant to hurt my feelings. She said she was sorry and she looked sorry. I guess I was so mad I didn't believe her when she tried to apologize.

Rhonda's mother was a helpful listener. She saw Rhonda's facial expressions, observed Rhonda's actions, and sensed that something was bothering her. She listened to Rhonda and reflected back to her the pain she was feeling. Because of the empathy Rhonda's mother showed as she listened, Rhonda knew her mother cared about her, that she was sorry she was in pain, that she understood the feelings she was having, and that she accepted her need to express those feelings. Her mother's patient, noncritical listening encouraged Rhonda to express her feelings openly, work through her hurt feelings, and finally reach her own conclusion that Sharon had not meant to hurt her.

Take the Child's Feelings Seriously

Five-year-old Kevin runs screaming to his mother while holding his knee. His mother expects to find a large gash bleeding profusely beneath his pantleg. Upon examination she sees only a slightly red knee. She responds to her son's expression of his feelings with:

Kevin's mother does not take his feelings seriously. She sees no blood and decides he shouldn't feel hurt. Kevin is crying, however, not because of the scrape but because *his feelings are in pain.* His friend Nate pushed Kevin, did not help him up, and did not say he was sorry. Kevin feels rejected by Nate. Kevin's mother does not hear him saying that his feelings hurt more than his knee. Had Kevin's mother listened more carefully to what Kevin was really feeling she could have responded differently to his pain:

MOTHER: Oh, you fell on your knee. That hurts (She does not say what hurts. Obviously something hurts but she does not yet know what).

KEVIN: Nate did it. He pushed me.

MOTHER: It doesn't make you feel good when someone pushes you does it? (Mother suspects his feelings are hurt more than his knee.)

KEVIN: No, it makes me feel bad.

MOTHER: I'm sure it does. (Mother concludes that his feelings are in pain and takes those feelings seriously.)

Mother's responses show Kevin that she understands his pain and accepts it. Listening and responding to Kevin's real pain with empathy allows Kevin to quickly gain enough emotional strength to skip off and rejoin Nate in play.

Listen "Between the Lines" for Hidden Messages

Children do not always say exactly what they mean. Parents need to read between the lines to discover the child's true feelings. In the example which follows, Barbara, a competent fifth-grade student, is having trouble with fractions and pours out her feelings to her father. Barbara's father listens to what she says and skillfully reads the messages hidden between the lines.

Barbara dramatically complains, "I'm so stupid! I'll never understand this math. All the other kids learned it right away. I'm so dumb it takes me forever."

Barbara's father knows his daughter is not stupid and he doubts that her friends learned the math easier than she did. What then is Barbara really trying to say? How can her father respond in a helpful way? What Barbara needs is her father's empathy toward her *hidden feelings*. Barbara probably feels frustrated because she is not able to immediately grasp one particular math concept. A helpful response from her father might be, "This math page looks difficult. The book seems to be teaching something which is new to you. Let's see if we can figure out how to do this together."

This kind of parental response makes Barbara feel that her father understands how difficult and frustrating the math problems are, but that he believes she is capable of working through them with support and help from someone who cares about her. Her father's response to her feelings allowed Barbara to gain the emotional strength needed to approach the math problems with more confidence.

Listen and Respond with Empathy, Not with Judgments

One of the surest ways to stop the flow of communication between a parent and child is for the parent to adopt the role of judge of what is right and wrong with all the child says and does. Children are not looking for a judge when they share their feelings with parents. They are looking for someone who says, "I care about you and I'll try to understand what you are feeling."

Parents who judge their child's feelings negatively teach the child to keep his feelings to himself. The child quickly learns that there is something wrong with what he feels and suspects that there is also something wrong with him as a person. The child's self-concept suffers because he believes there is something wrong with him for possessing feelings condemned by his parents.

It is not necessary or realistic to think, however, that we will always agree with all our child's feelings. What is necessary and helpful to the child is that we recognize and accept his *need to possess and express these feelings.* When we empathize with our child's feelings rather than condemning or criticizing them, the child is given the opportunity to calm down and think more clearly about what has happened. He becomes better able to work through his troubled feelings and learn from frustrating situations, a process which reinforces his feelings of self-worth.

In the following example, Sally's mother listens with empathy as Sally tells of her after-school experience:

SALLY: I tore Mindy's coat.

MOTHER: You look upset about it.

SALLY: I am. She promised to wait for me but she didn't. She went off with some other kids.

MOTHER: That must have made you disappointed in her or even mad.

SALLY: I was mad. She shouldn't have done that.

MOTHER: When Mindy ran off without you, it hurt your feelings.

SALLY: That's why I grabbed her pocket, to pull her back.

MOTHER: That's when the pocket tore?

SALLY: I didn't mean to tear her pocket. I only wanted to let her know it was wrong to break a promise.

MOTHER: Did Mindy tell you why she didn't keep her promise?

SALLY: No, she won't even talk to me now. She's mad because I tore her coat.

MOTHER: It sounds like both of you are pretty upset over what happened.

Sally's mother does not lecture Sally about what she should have done in the situation. Instead, she listens with empathy. This helpful listening allows Sally the opportunity to express her feelings openly and work through the painful experience without thinking that something is wrong with her feelings or herself.

Compare the way judging-condemning versus empathetic-sensitive parents listen and respond to the child's feelings:

CHILD SAYS:	JUDGING-CONDEMNING PARENT SAYS:	PARENT RESPONDING WITH EMPATHY SAYS:
"I hate Mrs. White. She thinks she can boss everyone around."	"You shouldn't say that. You know you don't really hate her."	"It sounds like you are pretty mad about something she did."
"I'm never going to play with Chris again."	"Oh stop being so upset. You know very well you'll be right out there tomorrow with him."	"You don't sound too happy with Chris."
"You never let me do anything fun like Tina."	"That's not true. You get to do many fun things. You went swimming yesterday, didn't you?"	"You feel like Tina gets to have more fun than you. Is that right? Why do you feel that way?"

The way parents listen and respond to their child's feelings greatly affects the child's self-concept. Parents who listen and respond to their child's feelings with empathy, caring, and patience encourage the child to feel worthwhile, accepted, and loved. These feelings nurture a positive self-concept, open parent–child communications, and a quality parent–child relationship.

EMPATHETIC LISTENING CHECKLIST

The checklist below is intended to remind us of the importance of listening and responding with empathy to our children's feelings.

		Seldom	Some	Usually
1.	I encourage my child to express his feelings openly, assuring him that I am not there to make judgments about his feelings.			
2.	I take my child's feelings seriously and do not deny that he feels the way he does.			
3.	I try to really "tune in" to what my child is saying.			
4.	I listen to my child with patience, warmth, and caring.			
5.	I try to understand what my child might be feeling by attempting to put myself in his place, seeing things from his point of view.			
6.	I listen "between the lines" for hidden messages which my child may have difficulty expressing.			
7.	I respond to my child's feelings without lecturing, criticizing, or blaming.			
8.	My child knows that I always take time to listen to him attentively because I care about him and his feelings.			
9.	I listen to my child in a way that encourages him to feel accepted, competent, worthwhile, and loved.			
10.	I am an empathetic-sensitive listener rather than a judging-condemning listener.			

If many of your checks are found in the "Usually" column, you are probably a parent who listens and responds to his child's feelings in ways which allow him to develop good feelings about himself.

chapter 16

Being More Accepting of Yourself as a Parent

I have emphasized the importance of children possessing good feelings about themselves and the ways in which those feelings may determine the kinds of relationships they have with other people, including their brothers and sisters. Now, I will focus on the self-concepts of parents. Parents also have feelings about themselves, some positive and some negative, and the ways they feel about themselves greatly influences their children's self-concepts.

For example, Harold is an unhappy person who struggles to get through each day. He thinks he is not likeable, believes he has not accomplished anything of importance, and feels that his family cares more about the paycheck he brings home than they do about him.

In contrast, Shirley is a person who enjoys life. She believes that her husband and children love her and think she is special and productive. Most of the time Shirley feels like a worthwhile person who is respected and loved by those around her.

Shirley's positive self-concept affects the way she greets each day and the way she interacts with people around her, including her children. Harold's negative self-concept also affects the relationships he develops with his children.

A child's self-concept is closely related to his parents' self-concepts. We can then cautiously predict that Harold's children possess low self-esteem. They are likely to feel incompetent, worthless, and unlovable, as he does. To determine the severity of those feelings would, of course, require closer examination. However, caution in predicting a child's self-concept is necessary. It must be remembered that both parents influence the child's self-concept, as do other people outside the home who interact with that child.

We can also predict, with caution, that Shirley's children possess positive feelings about themselves. Shirley's positive self-concept undoubtedly has an effect on the development of positive feelings in her children.

HOW DOES THE PARENT'S SELF-CONCEPT AFFECT THE CHILD'S SELF-CONCEPT?

Why does the condition of a child's self-concept often resemble that of his parent? The child does not inherit his self-concept from his parents. Rather, self-concept develops as the result of daily parent-child interactions. The diagram explains:

EFFECT OF PARENT'S SELF-CONCEPT ON CHILD'S SELF-CONCEPT

CONDITION OF PARENT'S SELF-CONCEPT:	The parent with a positive self-concept has good feelings about himself. He tends to view life, other people, and his children in a positive way.	The parent with a negative self-concept does not feel good about himself. He tends to view life, other people, and his children in negative ways.
PARENT'S BEHAVIOR TOWARD HIS CHILD:	The parent with a positive self-concept is more able and inclined to act in warm, supportive ways toward his child, because he feels good about himself.	The parent who sees himself negatively is less able and inclined to act in warm, supportive ways toward his child. Because he does not have positive feelings toward himself, he does not have positive, accepting feelings toward his child.
CHILD FEELS:	The child receiving supportive, positive responses from his parent learns that he is competent, worthwhile, and lovable. This encourages him to develop positive feelings about himself.	The child who receives negative messages from his parent is likely to feel incompetent, worthless, and unlovable. The development of a negative self-concept similar to that of his parent is probable.

LOVING OURSELVES

The parent's self-concept greatly influences the development of the child's self-concept. This being the case, one of the most effective ways to help our children develop positive feelings about themselves is to first develop more positive feelings about ourselves.

Like children, the quality of our self-concept depends upon images reflected to us by the significant people in our lives who give us information about what kind of person we are. If our environmental mirror, consisting of our husband or wife, close relatives, friends, and co-workers, sends verbal and nonverbal messages to us which say, "You are incompetent, not very worthwhile, and not lovable," we may believe those messages and view ourselves negatively. If, however, the people around us send messages which say "You are wonderful and are enjoyable to be around," we are apt to believe those messages and feel good about ourselves. Those positive feelings result in high self-esteem.

Adults as well as children need to have supportive, caring people around them who recognize their positive qualities and reflect an image to them which says, "You are skillful, worthwhile and lovable." Simple, positive messages mean a lot as the following example illustrates: A thirty-eight-year-old woman began jogging daily with her husband. After several months, her husband turned to her as they puffed down the road and said, "You know, you are a good runner." This grown woman swelled with pride. Despite the fact that she could not break a ten-minute mile, she saw herself as skillful at running and as a result felt slightly more competent and worthwhile. Her husband sent a helpful message to her which said, "You're an O.K. person," and helped her to feel good about herself.

The wife who leaves a note between the lettuce and pickle on her husband's sandwich which reads, "I'm glad you came home for lunch. I enjoy this time with you alone," may give her husband a pickle-soaked note, but she also gives him a message which says, "You are lovable. I enjoy being with you."

The four-year-old boy who drags a branch full of dried leaves onto a freshly vacuumed carpet, saying, "Love is when you bring your Mommy trees," is sending you the message, "I love you, Mommy. You mean a lot to me."

The way a person feels about himself changes from day to day. When the messages we receive from our environment fail to tell us we are competent, worthwhile, and lovable we may begin to feel that way inside.

For example, I know a woman who for seven years was totally absorbed in her work with young children and their parents in a nursery school program. It was an extremely rewarding experience, watching young children grow and develop and feeling that she was making a significant contribution to their development. She felt good when a little boy hugged her and said, "I love you, teacher," or a little girl climbed onto her lap and touched her cheek. The children in the school helped her to feel worthwhile and lovable. Their parents sought her advice, again making her feel that her opinion was valuable. The children and parents gave her daily doses of "You're O.K." medicine. She had very positive feelings about herself.

Then, something happened in this woman's life to keep her from receiving those daily doses of "You're O.K." medicine from those people with whom she worked. She took a year's leave from the school while she worked on a book entitled, *Quarreling Kids*. She discovered that facing a typewriter six hours a day is lonely. The writing was hard and sometimes she wasn't sure she could complete the book. She began to question her competency. No children or parents sent her messages which told her she was competent, worthwhile and lovable. The typewriter never once wrote, "I love you, teacher," or hugged her so she would feel lovable. Her new work environment provided few positive messages. Although her new occupation did not offer positive messages to her, this woman had a husband, children, and friends who were sensitive to her needs and continued to give her messages which made her feel worthwhile. Thus, her story ends happily.

IMPROVING OUR OWN SELF-CONCEPT

If the messages we receive from those around us are positive, listening to those messages and believing them will help to improve our self-concepts. However, if people around us aren't sending warm, supportive messages, we must improve our own self-concept.

We shall touch on some ideas which parents may find helpful in learning how to see themselves more positively. All the strategies suggested are designed for persons who function within a normal range and would like to function more effectively. In contrast, people who have strong feelings of sadness may find counseling beneficial.

Strategy—"My Good Side"

Most adults have a natural tendency to focus on all the things wrong with them. What we must do, instead, is make a concerted effort to discover all the positive things about ourselves. One strategy which has proven helpful to some adults in their efforts to see themselves more positively is called "My Good Side." The objective of this strategy is to focus on those things about us which suggest that we are competent, worthwhile, and lovable.

Directions: Make a list of 15 items which give evidence that you are competent, worthwhile, and lovable. List items which you consider big (I am a good sounding board for my husband), and small (I play ping pong well). Only positive items are permitted. Don't be tentative in your answers (I'm kind of good at playing the guitar).

"MY GOOD SIDE"

1.	9.
2.	10.
3.	11.
4.	12.
5.	13.
6.	14.
7.	15.
8.	

During a personal growth workshop for parents, I asked participants to work on "My Good Side." The participants groaned in unison, and comments floated about the room, such as "My list certainly is going to be short." Most agreed it was difficult to think of 15 items which gave evidence that they were competent, worthwhile, and lovable.

One parent said, "I feel uncomfortable thinking about my good points. It's as though I'm bragging or self-centered. It doesn't feel right to love myself." This parent's feelings are not unusual, which is unfortunate because the ability to accept and love oneself greatly affects the ability to show warmth, support and love to others, including our children. We become better parents and are able to interact with our children in more positive ways when we accept and love ourselves.

Strategy—"Two Years from Now, I . . ."

Few people feel they have used all their potential to the fullest and are 100% competent, worthwhile, and lovable all the time. Most people feel there is room for some growth in their lives. What can we do to grow, to learn to feel good about ourselves and to believe we are competent, worthwhile, and lovable? People do not grow by stating simply, "I accept myself. I love myself." Instead, we must define carefully those things which we value, and set upon a course which will help us to obtain those valued attributes.

Directions: Imagine what you would like your life to look like two years from now. What do you want to be doing? What do you want your relationships to be with your spouse, children, friends? What feelings do you want to have about yourself? In this strategy, you will define what you value by writing about how you would like to see yourself in two years. Your list may include personal accomplishments, relationships with other people, physical appearance, and so on.

Example: Two years from now I *want to get a job typing,* or Two years from now I *want to have a closer, more meaningful relationship with my daughter.*

"TWO YEARS FROM NOW, I . . . "

1. Two years from now I _____

2. Two years from now I _____

3. Two years from now I _____

4. Two years from now I _____

5. Two years from now I _____

6. Two years from now I _____

7. Two years from now I _____

8. Two years from now I _____

9. Two years from now I _____

10. Two years from now I _____

Strategy—"First Steps"

If our dreams are realistic ones we can make them happen. However, if tomorrow we go through the day as we always have, our dreams for two years from now probably won't come true. Instead, we must develop a game plan for making things happen in our lives which we value, and take some important "first steps" in those directions. The objective of "First Steps" is to plan, in writing, what those first steps will be.

Directions: Select at least five items from your "Two Years from Now, I . . ." list. Choose some specific things you can do tomorrow which will start you toward those goals. Write specifically what those steps will be.

Example: Two years from now I *want to have a closer, more meaningful relationship with my daughter.* First Steps—I will become a better listener and show her I really care about her life and want to share it. Tomorrow, I will ask her to take a walk with me. I will tell her how much she means to me and try to really listen to what she is saying.

"FIRST STEPS"

1. Two years from now I _____
   First Steps _____

2. Two years from now I _____
   First Steps _____

3. Two years from now I _____
   First Steps _____

4. Two years from now I _____
   First Steps _____

5. Two years from now I _____
   First Steps _____

These first few steps we take are the most important in helping us to take charge of our lives, to consciously become the kind of person we value, and begin to feel more competent, worthwhile, and lovable. These first steps must be followed by continued thinking about where we want to go and moving in those directions. A personal log in which we remind ourselves daily or weekly of our goals and the steps we must take to accomplish them can help us sustain positive growth. By becoming more accepting of ourselves, we become more accepting of our children and are more able to allow and encourage them to develop positive feelings about themselves.

chapter 17

Discipline and the Child's Self-concept

One of the greatest concerns of parents is discipline. Parents want their children to be "well-disciplined" but often aren't sure exactly what that means or how to go about making it happen. They know the dangers of being overly permissive, allowing the child to do anything he or she wants, and, at the other extreme, being authoritarian, dictating the child's every move. Sometimes parents decide to stay somewhere in the middle. This may mean being lax on discipline one minute and very strict the next.

Inconsistency in disciplining children may show itself in a variety of ways: father disciplines one way while mother another; what is considered to be okay behavior one day is not okay behavior the next; harsh, restrictive controls on the child's behavior one time, and a lenient, "do-your-own-thing" attitude toward the child's behavior the next time.

Studies have repeatedly shown that a high incidence of erratic or inconsistent discipline contributes to antisocial behavior. Wesley C. Becker concludes that: "This inconsistent discipline apparently contributes to maladjustment, conflict, and aggression in the child" (Becker, 1964, p. 200). This inconsistency in the type of discipline used by parents often occurs because parents are uncertain as to what type of discipline is best for their children.

WHAT KIND OF DISCIPLINE SHALL WE USE?

The kind of discipline we use with our children greatly affects the development of their self-concept. Some forms of discipline make children feel inadequate, worthless, and unloved. The kind of discipline most parents would want to use with their children is one which:

1. allows and encourages the child to develop good feelings about himself (positive self-concept) while
2. helps the child learn to behave in socially acceptable ways.

Let us look at three types of discipline and their effects upon children's self-concepts and behavior: *authoritarian, permissive,* and *constructive.*

EFFECTS OF AUTHORITARIAN DISCIPLINE ON THE CHILD'S SELF-CONCEPT AND BEHAVIOR

Parents are the power figures in authoritarian discipline. They make the rules which the child is expected to follow. The child has no input into what those rules will be. His role is to follow the rules, not question them. The parents manip-

Authoritarian Discipline

ulate the child's behavior through the use of rewards and punishments to assure that the rules are followed.

Is Authoritarian Discipline Effective in Controlling Behavior?

The consistent use of authoritarian discipline is sometimes effective in controlling children's behavior. Young children, especially, desperately need approval from their parents and will comply with their dictates in order to receive that approval. As long as the parent is nearby, scrutinizing the child's behavior, he will follow the rules. When out of parents' view, however, some children will "cut loose" and behave in ways which do not meet with their parents' approval.

As children grow older and less dependent on their parents, they may begin to ignore their parents' dictated boundaries. Instead, they choose behaviors which win for them the approval of their peers and other significant people in their lives. Parents are often shocked at this changed behavior. They have difficulty understanding why "he used to be such a good boy and now, all of a sudden, he rebels against everything we say." The more restrictive the boundaries set for the child by his parents, the more the child feels an overwhelming need and temptation to step over those boundaries, though seldom in front of his parents.

Even though authoritarian discipline may prove effective in controlling children's behavior in some instances, its use often results in harmful consequences which threaten the emotional well-being of the child. Authoritarian discipline and parent-dictated boundaries may cause children to react with defiance, negativism, resentment, anger, lying, sneaking, and aggressive behaviors. Or, children may submit to their parents' dictates while withdrawing, regressing, and becoming passive and fearful.

To raise self-disciplined children is the goal of most parents. They want their children to learn how to be responsible for their own behavior. Children growing up under strict authoritarian discipline have no opportunity to develop self-discipline. Children are not taught how to set constructive boundaries for themselves nor are they given the opportunity to learn how to monitor their own behavior when authoritarian discipline is used by their parents. Instead, authoritarian discipline teaches the child to rely on external controls of his behavior.

Effects of Authoritarian Discipline on the Child's Self-concept

It was noted previously that authoritarian discipline may, in some instances be effective in producing well-behaved children. However, during the process of producing well-behaved children, authoritarian discipline teaches children to have negative feelings about themselves. As the parent demands certain behaviors of the child, rather than involving the child in the process of choosing appropriate behaviors, the parent delivers harmful messages to the child, messages which say: "You are not competent to run your own life. You are not capable of monitoring your own behavior. You are not an okay person." Such messages nurture a negative self-concept. For example:

AUTHORITARIAN DISCIPLINE CAUSES THE CHILD TO THINK:	THE CHILD CONCLUDES:	EFFECT ON CHILD'S SELF-CONCEPT:
My parents tell me what to do because I don't act right.	I'm not a responsible person.	negative
My parents watch every move I make because they don't trust me.	I'm not to be trusted.	negative
My parents try to change me because they do not approve of me as I am.	I'm not acceptable.	negative
If I rebel against their rules by lying or being defiant, they let me know I'm bad.	I'm a bad person. I'm not lovable.	negative
My parents don't think I can live my own life in an acceptable way.	I'm not competent.	negative

In these ways, authoritarian discipline causes the child to develop a negative self-concept. Children who have negative feelings about themselves have difficulty feeling good about others. Therefore, we often find troubled sibling relationships in homes which use strict authoritarian discipline. The troubled sibling relationships may be expressed in hostile, bitter quarreling. Even when no outward signs of sibling difficulties exist, because the authoritarian parent has punished such behavior, the children's poor self-concepts and troubled sibling relationships may remain.

EFFECTS OF PERMISSIVE DISCIPLINE ON THE CHILD'S SELF-CONCEPT AND BEHAVIOR

Over-permissive discipline allows the child to dictate the rules and boundaries of his behavior. The child receives no guidance from his parents or practice in setting constructive boundaries. He learns to manipulate his parents in order to fulfill his every desire.

Does Permissive Discipline Help Children Learn Socially Acceptable Behaviors?

Parents who are excessively permissive find they have little control over their child's behavior. They are unable to teach their child socially acceptable behaviors because the child has learned **not** to listen.

Permissive discipline encourages the child to be self-centered and demanding. The child tries on obnoxious behaviors and finds they work for him. If his parents allow him to

Permissive Discipline

feel comfortable in those obnoxious behaviors and fail to point out to him what is and what is not acceptable behavior, the child will continue to engage in socially unacceptable behaviors. Soon the parents find they have no influence on their child's behavior. The child has the power, and he decides how he will behave.

The child raised in a permissive environment demands instant gratification of all his desires. He is impulsive and demanding, and has little thought for others' feelings and needs. He is unable to accept boundaries established for the good of all.

The child who is not taught how to set constructive boundaries and live within them often chooses behaviors which are not generally considered socially acceptable. The child growing up in a permissive environment often becomes defiant, aggressive, and manipulative of others in order to continue to have his demands met. Permissive discipline does not teach the child socially acceptable behavior.

Effects of Permissive Discipline on the Child's Self-concept

The young child who has not learned socially acceptable behaviors from his parents will eventually be criticized by people in his expanded environment—teachers, neighbors, relatives, peers. The messages they send to him about his inappropriate behavior will cause him to develop negative feelings about himself. The case below provides an example:

Until Billy was six years old the people in his world consisted mainly of his parents and two older sisters. Billy was bright, cute, creative, and friendly.

At the dinner table he entertained everyone with his sense of humor, turning his napkin into a clown hat, tapping silverware on the table while singing the latest rock tune, eating mashed potatoes with his knife, and periodically letting out a loud belch which sent his sisters into hysterics. There was little time for other family members to contribute to the dinner conversation because Billy monopolized it. Billy was led to believe by those around him that his entertaining behaviors were acceptable. The reflections he received from his environmental mirror were positive, and he felt good about himself.

At the age of 6½ Billy entered first grade. New people were added to his environmental mirror: teachers, classmates, the bus driver and the lunchroom supervisor.

Billy's lunch room supervisor didn't approve of his tapping spoon, loud belches, and entertaining antics. She told him his behavior was not acceptable. The bus driver did not approve of Billy climbing over the seats and through the aisle. Billy's teacher did not appreciate his performing for classmates while she was conducting a reading group or his attempting to monopolize group-time discussions. She, too, informed Billy that his behavior was bad. Billy had difficulty with his peers. When he demanded someone get out of the swing, his classmates chanted, "spoiled kid, always has to have his way!"

Because of the negative messages being sent to Billy by the people in his environment, his self-concept was shaken and he was confused. He felt that these new people didn't like him and thought that something was wrong with him. Negative reports from Billy's teachers caused his parents to also feel Billy didn't behave properly. They, too, began to criticize him, and he felt he had lost their approval also.

When parents do not help their children learn acceptable behaviors, they are likely to adopt impulsive, self-centered, demanding behaviors which are eventually criticized by those around them. As a result they develop negative feelings about themselves. Permissive discipline is harmful to the child's self-concept.

EFFECTS OF CONSTRUCTIVE DISCIPLINE ON THE CHILD'S SELF-CONCEPT AND BEHAVIOR

Discipline which helps the child learn desirable behavior and encourages him to develop a positive self-concept depends on parent-child interaction. The child and parent share their thoughts with each other concerning what constitutes acceptable behavior.

"Constructive discipline" places the parent in the role of *teacher,* rather than that of *spectator* as in permissive discipline, or *dictator* as in authoritarian discipline. Constructive discipline consists of the following elements:

1. Adult-child interaction in determining boundaries so the child can learn *how* and *why* boundaries are set on behavior;

2. Setting of boundaries based on the child's needs and maturity (readiness to handle expanding boundaries successfully);

3. Boundaries which allow for manageable amounts of freedom while protecting the child from environmental elements which he is not yet able to handle successfully;

4. Opportunity for the child, as he becomes more mature, to practice setting boundaries on his own behavior, unaided by his parents.

What Are Constructive and Realistic Boundaries for Children's Behavior?

Determining constructive and realistic boundaries for children's behavior is not an easy task. Of necessity, the boundaries must change as the child's needs and maturity levels change. In addition, parents must exercise personal judgments as to what constitutes realistic boundaries — boundaries intended to safeguard the child's well-being. In making decisions regarding realistic boundaries for children, it is helpful to have an idea of what is "normal" behavior at various ages and stages of development.

For example, if parents know that it is very "normal" for adolescents to want to conform to their peer group's dress code, it is somewhat easier for them to accept their own children's leaving for school most mornings in faded blue jeans and dirty tennis shoes. Also, we can better understand why a ten-year-old often forgets his lunch box when we realize forgetfulness is "normal" behavior for children of this age, and nothing about which we need be overly concerned. I strongly encourage every parent to purchase a reliable resource book giving information about the growth and development of children from birth through adolescence.

One rule may be kept in mind for determining constructive and realistic boundaries:

> *My children are free and encouraged to follow their personal inclinations and interests as long as they do not infringe upon the rights of others or endanger their own well-being.*

This rule permits the setting of boundaries which allow the child great amounts of freedom while protecting him from environmental elements which he is not yet capable of handling. For example, a three-year-old would not be free to cross the highway by himself because he is not yet able to handle this experience safely. This rule takes into consideration the child's need to have room to be free, explore, create, learn, and grow, while providing protection for him within secure and safe boundaries. Children can learn to use this one rule in guiding their own behavior, rather than trying to follow many other rules which may appear to change depending upon the moods of the parents.

Children will feel comfortable with decisions based on

this rule (whether initiated by the parent or child) if they see the rule itself as fair and reasonable. Practice in applying the rule through parent-child interaction helps the child realize that there are reasons for decisions, based on respecting the needs of parents and children. How does the rule work?

> *Six-year-old Greg wants to wash the car. The day is sunny and Father doesn't need the car during the next hour. Can Greg wash the car?* **Application of rule**—*Yes, it is safe and he is not infringing on anyone's rights.*

> *Six-year-old Greg wants to wash the car. The temperature is 35° and Father must leave for a meeting in ten minutes. Can Greg wash the car?* **Application of rule**—*No, the low temperature increases Greg's risk of catching a cold which endangers his well-being. Furthermore, the car's remaining home for a wash would infringe on Father's right to attend his meeting on time.*

> *Fifteen-year-old Brad wants to practice his baritone at ten o'clock at night. The rest of the family has gone to bed. Can Brad practice?* **Application of rule**—*No, if it means keeping others awake and infringing on their right to needed sleep. Yes, if Brad can find a place to practice where it will not keep others awake (perhaps in the garage).*

Unfortunately, this concise, reasonable-sounding rule is not always so easy to use. Consider these more difficult situations:

> *Twelve-year-old Nancy wants to have her girlfriends for a slumber party Friday night. Her parents have made prior commitments for dinner out that evening. Can Nancy have a slumber party?*

> **Application of rule**—*If Nancy's parents cancel their dinner plans, their rights to have an enjoyable evening out have been infringed upon. However, Nancy also has a right to plan fun*

times with her friends. This does not, however, necessarily mean instant fulfillment of that right. The conflict is settled fairly when Nancy chooses another evening for her slumber party.

Laura and her brother Paul own a skateboard between them. Both want to use the skateboard Saturday morning. Who gets to use the skateboard?

Application of rule—*Paul or Laura do not have the right to exclusive use of the skateboard owned by both. It would be an infringement on one child's rights to permit the other to exclusive use of the skateboard. The rights of both children can be protected by working out a compromise. There are a number of ways the children may negotiate a compromise while considering the needs and rights of each other: a) Each child uses the skateboard two hours Saturday morning; b) One child uses the board this Saturday, the other child next Saturday; c) If using the skateboard all of Saturday morning is of extreme importance, the children may need to work out a weighted settlement, such as Laura's using the board all of this Saturday in return for Paul's using the board during the next two weeks.*

Children need to learn that they do not always have the right to instant gratification of their needs and rights. It is sometimes necessary for the fulfillment of their needs to be delayed. Also, compromise may be necessary to ensure that the needs and rights of all involved are considered and dealt with fairly.

Unfortunately, there will be times when the parent and child will not agree upon what are fair and reasonable boundaries and acceptable behavior. What happens then?

After listening patiently to seven-year-old Jill's insistence that she is big enough to ride her two-wheeler in the street like the neighbor child, her parents' judgment still remains the same —Jill is not mature enough to assure that she will ride her bike in the street safely.

Jill and her parents disagree on whether bike riding in the street endangers her well-being. Should Jill be allowed to ride her bike in the street with her friend of the same age? No!

Application of rule—*When children's judgments are not realistic due to their age and maturity, parents must make the decision, even though it is not acceptable to the child. Parents have the responsibility to protect their children from environmental elements which they are not yet capable of handling successfully.*

In these difficult situations, where parents are forced to "pull rank" and use their power, it is important that the parents explain why they have made their decision and empathize with the child's frustration in not getting his or her way: "Jill, I know it is hard not to be able to ride your bike in the street when Shelly gets to. I'm sorry that you have to be disappointed. We believe it is dangerous for children your age to ride in the street. We want to be sure you are safe, so we cannot allow you to ride in the street with Shelly. Someday, when you are older, you will be able to ride in the street safely by yourself. However, you may ride in the street if your mother or I are with you."

Does Constructive Discipline Help Children Learn Socially Acceptable Behaviors?

Constructive discipline teaches the child how to set boundaries for his own behavior and why such boundaries are necessary. It gives the child the opportunity to practice setting self-boundaries and be actively involved with his parents in the process. Consequently, he has less difficulty living within those defined boundaries, and learns to monitor his own behavior responsibly. (Constructive discipline enables the child to become self-disciplined and learn socially acceptable behavior.)

Effects of Constructive Discipline on the Child's Self-concept

While simultaneously allowing him freedom to explore, create, learn, and grow, constructive discipline teaches the child socially acceptable behavior. Reflections from the people in his environment send messages to him which say: "You are competent, worthwhile, lovable, have acceptable behavior, and are an okay person." These positive reflections nurture a positive self-concept.

WHAT KIND OF DISCIPLINE SHALL WE USE?

The chart below and on the following page summarizes the effects of authoritarian, permissive, and constructive discipline on children's behavior and self-concepts:

Kinds of Discipline

	AUTHORITARIAN DISCIPLINE	PERMISSIVE DISCIPLINE	CONSTRUCTIVE DISCIPLINE
DESCRIPTION	Parent dictates boundaries; Parent enforces boundaries; Child not taught how to set boundaries on own behavior; Child not permitted to monitor own behavior.	Child dictates boundaries; Child not taught how to set healthy boundaries; Child not able to monitor own behavior.	Parent-child interaction in determining boundaries; Child taught how to set boundaries on own behavior; Child given practice in monitoring own behavior.

	AUTHORITARIAN DISCIPLINE	PERMISSIVE DISCIPLINE	CONSTRUC-TIVE DISCIPLINE
EFFECT ON CHILD'S BEHAVIOR	Child becomes rebellious, defiant, negative, aggressive, unmanageable, engages in unacceptable behavior; Or, child reacts by withdrawing, regression, fear, blind obedience; Child has little self-discipline.	Child demands instant gratification, impulsive, self-centered, no inner control; Child may become defiant, aggressive, manipulative of others; Child has little self-discipline.	Child behaves in socially acceptable ways; Child has little difficulty living within boundaries; Child regulates his own behavior; Child is self disciplined.
REFLECTIONS FROM ENVIRONMENTAL MIRROR	Child behaves badly; Child is not responsible for his behavior; Child is mean and negative; Child is not an O.K. person; Or, child is dependent, afraid, dull.	Child is spoiled, unmanageable, irresponsible, selfish, immature, self-centered; Child behaves badly.	Child is well-behaved, creative, responsible, enjoyable to be around, sensitive to others' feelings and needs; Child is liked by adults and peers.
EFFECT ON CHILD'S SELF-CONCEPT	Child sees himself as not competent, worthwhile, or lovable; Child believes he is not an O.K. person.	Child sees himself as not competent, worthwhile, or lovable; Child believes he is not an O.K. person.	Child sees himself as competent, worthwhile, and lovable; Child believes he is an O.K. person.

The kind of discipline we use with our children greatly affects the development of their self-concept. "Constructive discipline" which is based on parent-child interaction fosters the development of positive self-concepts.

DISCIPLINE CHECKLIST

The checklist below can indicate to parents whether or not they use a constructive form of discipline with their children which encourages the development of positive self-concepts and socially acceptable behavior.

		Seldom	Some	Usually
1.	My child and I work together on setting boundaries for "desirable" behavior (parent-child interaction).			
2.	I try to get my child to behave by punishing his bad behavior. He knows that he must mind or suffer the consequences.			
3.	Considering his age, my child does a good job of controling his own behavior without my constant monitoring.			
4.	When my child demands instant gratification of his needs, I immediately comply so as not to frustrate him.			
5.	I try to help my child understand *why* boundaries are necessary. I help him learn to set his own constructive boundaries.			
6.	I control my child's behavior by setting strict rules and enforcing those rules to the letter.			
7.	With patience and guidance I allow my child to practice setting boundaries on his own behavior.			
8.	It is hard to know what kind of discipline to use, so I find myself being lax on discipline one minute and strict the next.			

	Seldom	Some	Usually
9. I want my child to be "well-disciplined" and try to accomplish this by encouraging those behaviors in *positive* ways.			
10. I believe my child should simply follow our rules and not ask *why* such rules exist.			
11. The kind of discipline I use with my child allows and encourages him to develop good feelings about himself.			
12. The discipline I use with my child causes him to feel like a "bad" person.			

Interpretation. If you responded to the above statements with checks in the "usually" column for odd-numbered statements and checks in the "seldom" column for even-numbered statements, you are probably a parent who uses a constructive form of discipline. You give your child the opportunity to engage in socially acceptable behavior while developing positive feelings about himself.

The Greatest Gift

Children can develop warm, loving sibling relationships and it all begins with a special gift from parents:

THE GREATEST GIFT OF LOVE A PARENT CAN GIVE HIS CHILD IS A POSITIVE SELF-CONCEPT.

BIBLIOGRAPHY

Becker, Wesley C. "Consequences of Different Kinds of Parental Discipline." In Hoffman, Martin and Lois Hoffman, ed. *Review of Child Development Research, Vol. I.* New York: Russell Sage Foundation, 1964.

Branden, Nathaniel. *The Psychology of Self-esteem.* New York: Bantam Books, 1969.

Briggs, Dorothy Corkille. *Celebrate Your Self.* New York: Doubleday, 1977.

Briggs, Dorothy Corkille. *Your Child's Self-Esteem.* Garden City, N.Y.: Doubleday, 1975.

Button, Alan Dewitt. *The Authentic Child.* New York: Random House, 1969.

Canfield, Jack and Harold C. Wells. *100 Ways to Enhance Self-Concept in the Classroom.* Englewood Cliffs, N.J.: Prentice-Hall, 1976.

Clanton, Gordon and Lynn G. Smith. *Jealousy.* Englewood Cliffs, N.J.: Prentice-Hall, 1977.

Combs, Arthur W. and Donald Snygg. *Individual Behavior, A Perceptual Approach to Behavior.* New York: Harper & Row, 1959.

Coopersmith, Stanley. *The Antecedents of Self-esteem.* San Francisco: W. H. Freeman & Company, Publishers, 1967.

Dinkmeyer, Don C. *Child Development, The Emerging Self.* Englewood Cliffs, N.J.: Prentice-Hall, 1965.

Felker, Donald W. *Building Positive Self-Concepts.* Minneapolis, Minn.: Burgess, 1974.

Forer, Lucille K. *Birth Order and Life Roles.* Springfield, Ill.: Chas C. Thomas, 1969.

Foster, J. C., F. L. Goodenough and J. E. Anderson. *The Sleep of Young Children.* Circular No. 4. Minneapolis: University of Minnesota, Institute of Child Welfare, 1930.

Fraiberg, Selma H. *The Magic Years.* New York: Scribner's, 1959.

Ginott, Haim. *Between Parent and Child.* New York: Macmillan, 1965.

Ginott, Haim. *Between Parent and Teen-ager.* New York: Macmillan, 1969.

Glasser, William. *Schools without Failure.* New York: Harper and Row, 1969.

Goodenough, Florence L. *Anger in Young Children.* Minneapolis, Minn.: The University of Minnesota Press, 1931.

Gordon, Thomas. *P.E.T. Parent Effectiveness Training.* New York: Peter H. Wyden, Inc., 1970.

Hamacheck, Don E., ed., *The Self in Growth, Teaching, and Learning.* Englewood Cliffs, N.J.: Prentice-Hall, 1965.

Hamacheck, Don E. *Encounters with the Self.* New York: Holt, Rinehart and Winston, Inc., 1971.

Hymes, James L. Jr. *A Child Development Point of View.* Englewood Cliffs, N.J.: Prentice-Hall, 1955.

Hymes, James L. Jr. *Behavior and Misbehavior.* Englewood Cliffs, N.J.: Prentice-Hall, 1955.

James, Muriel, and Dorothy Jongeward. *Born to Win.* Reading, Mass.: Addison-Wesley, 1971.

Jersild, Arthur T. *Child Psychology.* Englewood Cliffs, N.J.: Prentice-Hall, 1968.

Jersild, Arthur T. *In Search of Self.* New York: Teachers College Press, Columbia University, 1952.

Jersild, Arthur T. *When Teachers Face Themselves.* New York: Teachers College Press, Columbia University, 1955.

Jourard, Sidney M. *The Transparent Self.* New York: D.Van Nostrand, 1964.

Katz, Robert L. *Empathy.* New York: The Free Press of Glencoe, Macmillan, 1963.

Kennedy, J. F. *Profiles in Courage.* New York: Harper, 1956.

Lefkowitz, Monroe M. and others. *Growing up to be Violent: A Longitudinal Study of the Development of Aggression.* Elmsford, N.Y.: Pergamon Press, 1977.

LeShan, Eda J. *The Conspiracy Against Childhood.* New York: Atheneum, 1974.

LeShan, Eda J. *Natural Parenthood.* New York: Signet Books from New American Library, 1970.

Maslow, Abraham H. *Towards a Psychology of Being.* New York: Van Nostrand, 1962.

Missildine, W. Hugh. *Your Inner Child of the Past.* New York: Simon and Schuster, 1963.

Montagu, Ashley. *The Nature of Human Aggression.* New York: Oxford University Press, 1976.

Mussen, Paul and Nancy Eisenberg. *Roots of Caring, Sharing, and Helping, The Development of Prosocial Behavior in Children.* San Francisco: W. H. Freeman & Company Publishers, 1977.

Neisser, Edith G. *Brothers and Sisters.* New York: Harper and Brothers, 1951.

Neisser, Edith G. *The Eldest Child.* New York: Harper & Brothers, 1957.

Newman, Mildred, and Bernard Berkowitz. *How to Be Your Own Best Friend.* New York: Random House, 1971.

Otto, Herbert and John Mann, "Human Potential," in Herbert Otto (ed.), *Human Potentialities.* St. Louis: Warren H. Green, Inc., 1968.

Rogers, Carl R. *On Becoming a Person.* Boston: Houghton Mifflin Co., 1961.

Rothenberg, Michael B. "Television and Children," *Pediatrics in Review,* Vol. I, No. 10, April 1980.

Rubin, Theodore Isaac. *The Angry Book.* Toronto: Macmillan, Collier-Macmillan, Ltd., 1969.

Samuels, Shirley C. *Enhancing Self-concept in Early Childhood.* New York: Human Sciences Press, 1977.

Saul, Leon J. *The Psychodynamics of Hostility.* New York: Jason Aronson, Inc., 1976.

Simon, Sidney B. *Negative Criticism.* Niles, Ill.: Argus Communications, 1978.

Stone, Joseph L., and Joseph Church. *Childhood and Adolescence: A Psychology of the Growing Person,* 3rd ed. New York: Random House, 1968.

Sutton-Smith, Brian and B. G. Rosenberg. *The Sibling.* New York: Holt, Rinehart and Winston, 1970.

Toman, Walter. *Family Constellation, Its Effects on Personality and Social Behavior.* New York: Springer-Verlag, 1976.

Wickes, Frances G. *The Inner World of Childhood.* Englewood Cliffs, N.J.: Prentice-Hall, 1966.

Yamamoto, Kaoru. *The Child and His Image: Self-Concept in the Early Years.* Boston: Houghton Mifflin Co., 1972.

Ziman, Edmund. *Jealousy in Children, a Guide for Parents.* New York: Wyn, Inc., 1949.

Index

Acceptance
  of child, 156–58
  language of, 43–45, 160–68
Achievement
  parental pushing for, 36–39, 108–9,
    125
Adolescence
  lessening of overt signs of sibling
    rivalry, 19
  need for empathy, 160–68
Aggressiveness
  imitation of aggressive behaviors,
    57–59
  related to over-permissive
    discipline, 186
  as sign of jealousy, 28
  symptom of low self-esteem, 101
Anger
  causes of, 41, 101
  expressions of, 51–53, 66, 101

  handling constructively, 61–63
  indirect expressions of, 52–53
  learned ways to express, 53–63
  as normal, 55
  tantrums, 53
Anxiety
  related to low self-esteem, 101
Attention
  delayed, 155
  focused, 150–55
  lack of, 15
  negative, 152–53
  pretend, 153–54
  Quality Attention Checklist, 158–59
  quality attention (*See* Focused
    attention)
  substitute, 151–52
Authoritarian discipline, 181–84,
    193–94
  definition, 181–82

Peers
  pressure to conform, 39–40
  as role models, 57
Permissive discipline, 185–87
  definition, 185
  effect on children's behavior,
    185–86
  effect on child's self-concept, 186–87
  example of, 185–87
Personality of child as factor related
  to new baby acceptance, 23
Play, importance of, 124
Positive feelings (*See* Self-esteem)
Praise
  appreciative, 117
  desirable, 117
  effect on self-esteem, 115
Pressure on children, 36–41
  effects of, 37–40
  from parents, 36–37
  from peers, 39–40
  from teachers, 37–39
  pressuring techniques, 37
Pretend attention, 153–54
Productive children,
  development of, 135
Punishment
  in discipline, 181–82
  as pressuring technique, 37
  physical, 54
  verbal beatings, 54
Pushing
  for achievement, 111–12, 123–24
  adolescence, 125
  dangers of, 66, 128, 145
  effect on self-esteem, 66, 128, 145
  effect on sibling quarrels, 37, 39–40
  from parents, teachers, peers,
    36–41
  preschool children, 123–24
  pushing versus encouraging
    children, 126–27
  *Encouraging Versus Pushing
    Checklist,* 128–30

**Quality attention (*See* Focused
  attention)**
Quality parent-child relationship
  accepting and cherishing your child,
    156–58

  conditions for, 147–48
  definition, 147
  development of, 148
  giving focused attention, 150–51,
    154–55
  knowing your child, 148–50
  "Getting to Know You" strategy,
    148–50
Quarreling (*See* Quarrels)
  causes of, 1–67, 100–3, 105
  inability to express anger
    constructively, 51–63
  parental intervention, 61–63
  parent's role in helping children
    learn to quarrel less, 9–10, 17,
    61–83, 105–6
  related to home atmosphere, 41–46
  related to jealousy, 12
  related to physical causes: hunger,
    illness, fatigue, 47–50
  related to pressure from parents,
    peers, teachers, 36–40
  related to self-concept, 43, 64–67,
    100–6
  as symptom of underlying
    difficulties, 9, 47–50
Quarrels (*See* Quarreling)
  amount, 4
  common, 3–4
  comparison of three types of, 8
  destructive quarrels, 7–9 (*See*
    Destructive quarrels)
  emotional intensity of, 7–9
  factors related to quarreling:
    age of children, 19–20
    sex of children, 16–17
    birth order of children, 14–16
    spacing of children, 17–19
  harmful effects of, 4, 7–9
  means of expressing anger, 51–53
  nuisance quarrels, 5–6, 8 (*See*
    Nuisance quarrels)
  as source of useful information
    about children's feelings, 9–10
  as symptoms of underlying
    difficulties, 9–19
  three types of, 5–9 (*See* Nuisance
    quarrels, Destructive quarrels,
    Verbal debate quarrels)
  verbal debate, 6–8 (*See* Verbal
    debate quarrels)